But If Not

But If Not

WHEN BAD THINGS THREATEN TO DESTROY GOOD PEOPLE

Joyce and Dennis Ashton

CFI

Springville, Utah

This is not an official publication of The Church of Jesus Christ of Latter-day Saints. The opinions and views expressed herein belong solely to the author and do not necessarily represent the opinions or views of Cedar Fort, Inc. Permission for the use of sources, graphics, and photos is also solely the responsibility of the author.

ISBN 13: 978-1-59955-166-1

Published by CFI, an imprint of Cedar Fort, Inc., 2373 W. 700 S., Springville, UT 84663
Distributed by Cedar Fort, Inc., www.cedarfort.com

LIBRARY OF CONGRESS CATALOGING-IN-PUBLICATION DATA

    Ashton, Joyce.
     But if not : when bad things threaten to destroy good people / Joyce and
    Dennis Ashton.
       p. cm.
     ISBN 978-1-59955-166-1
     1. Suffering—Religious aspects—Church of Jesus Christ of Latter-day
    Saints. 2. Suffering—Religious aspects—Mormon Church. I. Ashton, Dennis,
    1950- II. Title.

    BX8643.S93A83 2008
    248.8'6—dc22

                2008010772

Cover design by Jeremy Beal
Cover design © 2008 by Lyle Mortimer

Printed in the United States of America

10 9 8 7 6 5 4 3 2 1

Printed on acid-free paper

IN MEMORY OF

Vivian Johnson Marsden

MY ANGEL MOTHER

1925–2008

CONTENTS

PREFACE

As I finished the final spell check for this volume of *But If Not: When Bad Things Threaten to Destroy Good People*, my angel mother slept nearby. She had been in our home on hospice for the past three months, dying of breast cancer complicated with end-stage dementia.

Dennis and I learned about loss and grief early in our marriage when we experienced infertility, followed by the death of our first full-term baby. We started writing about grief years later after the death of our disabled fourteen-year-old son, Cameron. Additional losses and life's challenges have inevitability continued to roll into our family's lives—miscarriage, disability, death, addiction, illness, and other life challenges. As we sadly watch our sweet mother take her last breaths, we simultaneously experience great joy as we plan for our youngest daughter's upcoming temple marriage.

Each of our lives are full of joy, loss, sadness, and hope, all weaved together. Our personal challenge is to remain faithful, find meaning, and choose to carry on in the face of our own inevitable unique trials and adversities. *But If Not* is offered as a guide and support as you cope with your own life challenges and losses. We wish you ultimate happiness and comfort on your life's journey. It is our hope and prayer that the lessons, techniques, and spiritual insights we have learned as fellow travelers will, in some beneficial way, ease your suffering.

—Joyce and Dennis Ashton

CHAPTER ONE

"But If Not ..."

IN SPITE OF THE JOYS AND BLESSINGS, life is full of challenges. For those rare individuals who haven't yet experienced a significant life challenge, we say, "Oh, they are still in the bubble!" The bubble can be compared to the Garden of Eden or an ideal world where there is no sadness, pain, or problems. We float innocently along as life unfolds exactly as planned. All of our choices and decisions provide us and those around us with perfect contentment and joy. No one is upset or disappointed. There is no sin. No one hurts or betrays us. All of our prayers are answered as we think they should be. We don't feel exhaustion or discouragement. Our children are obedient. We are cheerful, kind, and full of love, and we accept those around us. We are content with our uncomplicated life in the Garden of Eden. We know nothing different.

In the Garden of Eden, Adam and Eve "could not be agents unto themselves; for if they never should have bitter they could not know sweet" (D&C 29:39). However, even when we realize that we must know good from evil to "become as one" with God, it is no easy task (Moses 4:28; Genesis 3:22). Adam and Eve certainly experienced a significant adjustment when they first felt sweat on their brows and pain in their hearts.

As we venture out of our Garden of Eden, or when our bubble bursts, we will likely experience denial, shock, and sadness. We may attempt to find meaning as we wonder what has happened to us. At first we try to go back. We want things how they used to be. (Likely there were times when Adam and Eve longed to go back to the garden as well.) We desire everything to be the same again, at times even denying our new realities. We fight for what we consider normal, just, and deserved. As time passes, we sadly realize that we can never go back. We have heard that when one door closes another door opens. However, it is in the hallways where we wait and struggle![1] Our struggles and experiences become part of us and forever change how we look at the world and ourselves. We will likely never be the same again; however, we can find joy, meaning, and a "new normal" as we do our grief work.[2]

These concepts may be confusing for those around us who are still in the safe and peaceful Garden of Eden. They often attempt to justify why bad things have happened to others, but not them. They all too often contribute to another's pain by wrongly suggesting their suffering results from a lack of faith, will power, or motivation. Some judge silently, while others cry out that surely they must have somehow deserved their tragedy. Others bombard those in pain with all sorts of suggestions and clichés: "Perhaps you didn't pray or fast enough." "Where is your faith?" Or, "It must be God's will." Some conclude that those suffering must be guilty of an unrepented sin or have some other serious character flaw that is responsible for their pain and dysfunction.

Knowing good from evil and coming to understand the bitter and the sweet can result from a variety of life challenges (Moses 6:55–56; 2 Nephi 2:11, 15). Perhaps your pain and disappointment came early in your life. Maybe you didn't feel loved as a child, or maybe you were abused.

It might have been as simple as realizing you were not born with as much talent, fame, or fortune as those around you. You may be surrounded by individuals who seem to be blessed with kinder and more faithful families. Others may have inherited greater intelligence or better looks than you.

Maybe you have addictions or live with someone who does. Perhaps your daughter became pregnant out of wedlock or you are unable to find a spouse. Maybe your husband has left you for another woman or even another man. Perhaps your parents got divorced even after you prayed, went on a mission, and placed their names on the temple prayer roll. Perhaps after years of infertility and miscarriages your only child died. It could be that your mission ended before the appointed time in spite of sincere efforts to overcome your unrelenting anxiety and chronic depression. You may live with illness, a disability, or chronic pain. Maybe you were there in the last natural disaster or terrorist attack that has left you without home, employment, or family. Any of these significant life challenges and losses can leave you with heartache, disappointment, and grief. To heal and find meaning, you will likely need to do what is coined by some as "grief work." Grief work is often the hardest work we will ever do.

The scriptures confirm the reality that bad things happen to good people.[3] God "maketh his son to rise on the evil and on the good, and sendeth rain on the just and on the unjust" (Matthew 5:45).

The scriptures also give ample evidence that good people must endure hard times. Moses had to leave his comfortable life to accomplish what the Lord required of him (Exodus 4). Joseph Smith endured significant physical and emotional pain. Job suffered the loss of family, wealth, and health, and did not quickly find relief. He struggled emotionally with anger, anxiety (Job 3:25), and depression (Job 10:1). One of his losses resulted in spiritual injury as the heavens seemed silent. He questioned why God didn't hear and respond to his faithful, sincere pleadings (Job 30:20).

In the midst of Job's long and intense suffering, he asked the profound question, "If a man die, shall he live again?" (Job 14:14). Then, answering his own question, he gave us a key to find peace amid adversity with this testimony: "For I know that my redeemer liveth, and . . . though after my skin worms destroy this body, yet in my flesh shall I see God" (Job 19:25–6). And, "though he slay me, yet will I trust in him" (Job 13:15). Job's losses were restored to him before his death. Elder Bruce R. McConkie taught, "Anything that befalls us here in mortality is but for a small moment, and if we are true and faithful God will eventually exalt us on high. All our losses and sufferings will be made up to us in the resurrection."[4]

Jacob was another great prophet who suffered much loss. He worked seven years for Rachel, only to receive Leah and a requirement of seven more years of work for Rachel (Genesis 29). Rachel suffered years of infertility and then died after the birth of Benjamin, her second son (Genesis 35). Jacob was so grief stricken he said, "For I will go down into the grave unto my son mourning" (Genesis 37:35). More grief and shame was wrought upon Jacob when his daughter Dinah fornicated with an uncircumcised Hivite man. This angered Jacob's sons Simeon and Levi, who then murdered Dinah's lover as well as other males in the Hivite city (Genesis 34). Jacob was again grief stricken.

President Kimball also endured severe trials. Much of what he learned was through his own multiple losses and sufferings. He, like Job, suffered with boils. He also experienced skin cancer, Bell's palsy, smallpox, and heart pain for years that required open-heart surgery. He endured three brain surgeries and suffered skin and throat cancer, which necessitated vocal cord surgery requiring treatments and resulting in his difficulty of speech.[5]

We may logically understand that bad things can and often do happen to good people. However, when we actually experience a serious crisis firsthand, we may find it difficult to accept or believe that a significant tragedy has actually happened to us. We may ask, "Why me?" "Did I do something wrong?" Or we may reason, "I have faith, I have lived a good life, why can't I handle this better?" One such woman facing a serious challenge was told, "People of real faith don't have trials or crises." The statement caused her a great deal of spiritual injury and hurt.

Most of us are not prepared to understand or deal with all the emotions that flood us. We may have been taught falsely that if we are righteous and faithful, we can avoid serious pain and loss. We might also believe that when something difficult does happen to us, our faith, obedience, and prayer will protect or shield us from having to endure emotional or physical pain. It may be especially confusing for those who have strong faith, believe in miracles, and strive to live the commandments, when they are not protected from tragedy. Unfortunately, not even the righteous are granted all they desire in their hearts or pray for. Many faithful individuals do not receive the miracle they sincerely and desperately seek. Others endure pain as a result of the misuse of agency or the destructive and sometimes sinful choices of others.

When assaulted by a personal tragedy, we may feel ashamed to openly admit our feelings and disappointments to others, or sometimes even to ourselves. Consequently, we may choose to mask our true feelings in order to save face. We may pretend for long periods of time to be functioning well, all in a desperate attempt to fool others and ourselves. This facade is often reinforced and buried even deeper when others compliment us with statements such as, "You are so strong and doing so well." Our desire not to disappoint others precludes us from sharing our real feelings and admitting that we are struggling and need help. We then are forced to grieve in the shadows. We become silent sufferers. We fear we will be judged negatively, especially if we somehow feel responsible for the adversity. Our guilt complicates the grieving process and causes us to feel shame and a perceived loss of control over our lives. Our grief can become "disenfranchised" when no one is aware of, allows, acknowledges, or understands our loss.

Enduring hardship over a long period of time can add to the difficulty. When the suffering goes on and on and we can't see an end in sight, we may experience spiritual injury (see chapter 3). This spiritual injury became a reality for many during the Lamanite and Nephite wars. In the Book of Mormon we read that "many had become hardened . . . and many were softened" because of the length and suffering that resulted from the many years of war. Our life's challenge is to maintain soft hearts and not become hardened (Alma 62:41).

We may feel forsaken at times like Job, who said, "I cry unto thee . . . and thou regardest me not" (Job 30:20). Or, we may experience confusion like Moses, who cried, "Lord, wherefore hast thou so evil entreated this people? Why is it that thou hast sent me . . .

neither hast thou delivered thy people" (Exodus 5:22–23). We may wonder why God has allowed us to fall into difficult situations. Even Christ felt forsaken and alone in Gethsemane. When He found His apostles asleep, He asked them, "Could ye not watch with me but one hour?" (Matthew 26:37). And later on the cross He asked His Father, "Why hast thou forsaken me?" (Matthew 27:46).

There may be times when our family and friends disappoint us by not supporting us the way we think they should. We may have to accomplish some of our Gethsemane work without them. Neal A. Maxwell said of such suffering, "There is, in the suffering of the highest order, a point reached—a point of aloneness—when the individual (as did the Savior on a much grander scale) must bear it, as it were, alone. Even the faithful may wonder if they can take any more or if they are in some way forsaken. Those who, as it were, stand at the foot of the cross, often can do so little to help absorb the pain and the anguish. It is something we must bear by ourselves in order that our triumph can be complete."[6] Some may repeat the scriptural pleading, "The Lord hath forsaken me, and my Lord hath forgotten me." Or they may need the reassurance from the Lord's promises to us: "But he will show that he hath not . . . yet I will not forget thee. . . . Behold I have engraven thee upon the palms of my hands" (1 Nephi 21:14–16). "I will not fail thee, nor forsake thee" (Joshua 1:5).

The Lord has assured us that He will be with us: "I will not leave you comfortless" (John 14:18). "Fear not, let your hearts be comforted . . . waiting patiently on the Lord" (D&C 98:1–2). The Savior is our example. He is "a man of sorrows, and acquainted with grief" (Isaiah 53:3). He said, "I have drunk out of that bitter cup which the Father hath given me" (3 Nephi 11:11). We too may have to drink from a bitter cup. The secret is to follow Christ's example and not become bitter. We must choose between two *B*s and be "better, not bitter."

We all cope in different ways. Our coping skills are just as unique as our thumbprints. There are several coping variables to consider. We will discuss these variables in detail along with interventions and self-help tools designed to increase our capacity to achieve healing. We especially want to emphasize the spiritual healing found in chapter 3. The Lord has promised His spirit and guidance: "And though the Lord give you the bread of adversity, and the water of affliction, yet shall not thy teachers be removed into a corner any more, but thine eyes shall see thy teachers: And thine ears shall hear a word behind thee saying, this is the way; walk ye in it, when ye turn to the right hand, and when ye turn to the left" (Isaiah 30:20–21).

Sometimes we do get our miracle and the Lord removes our adversity. However, more often the Savior will strengthen and enable us in our adversity. God may not remove our adversity, just as He didn't immediately deliver Alma and his people who were persecuted by Amulon. Instead, in Mosiah 24:14, He said, "I will ease the burdens which are put upon your shoulders, that even you cannot feel them on your backs." Alma the Younger, in Alma 31, discouraged with his preaching prayed "that [he] may have strength, that [he] may suffer with patience these afflictions" (Alma 31:31). In Isaiah 53 we are told that the Savior offers comfort and understanding because He is acquainted with grief. He learned to succor us through his own suffering. Now He can carry our sorrow. In Alma 7 the Savior says He can bear any pain, grief, or sickness.

Dennis and I, like most of you, have had a life of both joy and adversity. We cared for our disabled son, Cameron, for fourteen years. We experienced infertility and miscarriage. We raised another son trapped in addictions. We have learned how quickly life can leave us as we buried three of our four parents and two of our six children. Our oldest son, Darren, had a colon mass removed that resulted in severe complications and several major surgeries. Through suffering he came to appreciate more deeply a phrase from a favorite scripture that we quote to each other when one of us gets discouraged: "But if not."

The scripture tells a powerful story about three righteous and brave men. Shadrach, Meshach, and Abed-nego were to be thrown into a "burning fiery furnace" for worshipping God. They displayed their commitment and faith by responding: "Our God whom we serve is able to deliver us . . . *but if not*, be it known . . . that we will not serve thy gods, nor worship the golden image" (Daniel 3:18; emphasis added).

Elder Dennis E. Simmons reminds us,

> We must have the same faith as Shadrach, Meshach, and Abed-nego.
>
> Our God will deliver us from ridicule and persecution, *but if not.* . . . Our God will deliver us from sickness and disease, *but if not.* . . . He will deliver us from loneliness, depression, or fear, *but if not.* . . . Our God will deliver us from threats, accusations, and insecurity, *but if not.* . . . He will deliver us from death or impairment of loved ones, *but if not,* . . . *we will trust in the Lord.*
>
> Our God will see that we receive justice and fairness, *but if not.* . . . He will make sure that we are loved and recognized, *but if not.* . . . We will receive a perfect companion and righteous and obedient children, *but if not,* . . . *we will have faith in the Lord Jesus Christ, knowing that if we do all we can do, we will, in His time and in His way, be delivered and receive all that He has* (see D&C 84:35–38).[7]

President Hinckley reminds us of this kind of faith: "Faith is something greater than ourselves that enables us to do what we said we will do. To press forward when we are tired or hurt or afraid. To keep going when the challenge seems overwhelming and the course is uncertain."[8]

Elder W. Craig Zwick of the Seventy said, "We must trust in the Lord. If we give ourselves freely to Him, our burdens will be lifted and our hearts will be consoled."[9]

Elder Richard G. Scott reminds us to "trust in God . . . no matter how challenging the circumstance. . . . Your peace of mind, your assurance of answers to vexing problems, your ultimate joy depends upon your trust in Heavenly Father and His Son, Jesus Christ."[10]

Most of us can and will adapt to loss and life's challenges as we discover our "new normal."[11] Our spirits can come to the realization that we will find lasting peace and that "joy cometh in the morning" (Psalm 30:5).

Notes

1. Elizabeth Kubler-Ross and David Kessler, *Life Lessons: Two Experts on Death and Dying Teach Us about the Mysteries of Life and Living* (New York: Scribner, 2000), 19.
2. Rana K. Limbo and Sara Rich Wheeler, *When a Baby Dies: A Handbook for Helping and Healing* (La Crosse Lutheran Hospital/Gunderson Clinic, Ltd., 1986), xv.
3. Harold Kushner, *When Bad Things Happen to Good People* (New York: Avon Books, 1981).
4. Bruce R. McConkie, in Conference Report, Oct. 1976, 158–60; *Ensign*, Nov. 1976, 106–108.
5. James E. Faust, "The Blessings of Adversity," *Ensign*, Feb. 1998, 2–7.
6. Neal A. Maxwell, *All These Things Shall Give Thee Experience* (Salt Lake City: Deseret Book, 1979), 43.
7. Dennis E. Simons, "But If Not . . ." *Ensign*, May 2004.
8. Gordon B. Hinckley, *Standing for Something* (New York: Times Book, 2000), 111.
9. W. Craig Zwick, "The Lord Thy God Will Hold Thy Hand," *Ensign*, May 2003.
10. Richard G. Scott, "The Sustaining Power of Faith in Times of Uncertainty and Testing," *Ensign*, May 2003.
11. Limbo and Wheeler, ibid.

CHAPTER TWO

Loss and Grief

GRIEF IS WHAT WE EXPERIENCE WHEN we lose something. Grief is work. It is the work of thoughts and feelings. It is how we heal from loss. In the beginning phase of loss and grief, we may not have much control over our thoughts or feelings. However, as we acknowledge and actually pursue our grief work, using the tools we will discuss in chapters 3 and 4, we can gain increased control and peace. We will probably still have unexpected experiences with grief, especially during holidays and at other significant times. However, by doing our grief work, we are choosing to be a survivor rather than a victim of our circumstances.

No two people's reactions following a crisis will be the same. The type of loss is one factor. Individual circumstances, former life experiences, and previous loss exposure are a few additional factors that contribute to our particular grief process.

Rana K. Limbo and Sara Rich Wheeler, authors of *When a Baby Dies*, teach, "Grief cannot be compared, measured, or quantified. . . . Healing . . . does not mean a quick cure; healing is putting the loss in perspective."[1]

The Chinese symbol for *crisis* consists of two figures: danger and opportunity. Crisis and adversity provide us with an opportunity to transform our pain into healing.

Most of us have had a physical injury. Healing from some physical injuries can take months or years, and often we are never quite the same. When we say someone can heal from a tragic event, or from a major loss that assaults both body and soul, we need to remember that it takes time and they will likely never be exactly the same again. Their loss becomes part of who they are, and although they can find joy and happiness again, they are different people. They see from a different perspective. Many use the term *recovery* when referring to this process. However, it may be more accurate to say that we reconcile, accommodate, or adjust to our loss.

Because most members of the Church depend on their spiritual strength and religious beliefs to get them through difficult challenges, our next chapter on spiritual healing can be especially important and relevant to them. We are blessed to have the gospel and the gift of the Holy Ghost. Christ offers us comfort and healing even when our adversity is not removed. While our faith and spiritual impressions bring great peace, it is also helpful to utilize and apply additional truths and knowledge inherently entwined in the grief process. These additional healing principles and processes can help us cope with loss and find personal meaning.

Individuals experiencing loss will be affected across the following five dimensions: spiritual, physical, social, emotional, and cognitive/intellectual. We will discuss the possible myriad grief symptoms in each of these areas. Additionally we will illustrate how each of the five dimensions interacts and affects the others.

Emotional Symptoms Resulting from Adversity and Loss

One of life's most meaningful emotions, happiness, is often compromised for a time by serious adversity and loss. Symptoms that are associated with acute grief include disbelief, denial, shock, and numbness.

SHOCK, NUMBNESS, AND DISBELIEF

"How can this be? I can't believe it is really happening!" Your assumptive world has been violated. This is not what you wanted or expected. You may want to say, "Life is not fair!" or "Why me?"

You may feel numb or in a state of confusion. The disbelief may initially overpower you. It may be difficult to experience happiness, joy, love, or spirituality for some time. It may be difficult to concentrate on even simple tasks. Your normal coping behaviors become depleted. The depth of your grief is often proportional to the depth of your love and time previously invested in those things or loved ones we have lost. The quality and quantity of your love, time, and service (emotional investment) may coincide with the difficulty and duration of your grief. Grief often takes more time, patience, and energy than most expect or feel capable of enduring.

DENIAL

For some of us, denial may remain for weeks, months, or even years. Sometimes friends and relatives contribute to this denial. They may reason, "Let's not bring it up or talk about it and maybe it will go away." Some may experience a deeper level of denial in their attempt to cope. This is called repression. It is an unconscious forgetting of the traumatic event. We may stuff the loss far from our conscious memory. Unfortunately, emotions not dealt with on a conscious level may appear as physical illness, generalized anxiety, panic attacks, or post-traumatic stress syndrome.

Some individuals use avoidance patterns to deny their grief. These are behaviors and attitudes that cause individuals to delay feeling pain. Avoidance patterns include purposely postponing, displacing, or minimizing the emotions or event. Some become obsessed with shopping, working, eating, intellectualizing, traveling, exercising, crusading, or drugging their pain.

There may be secondary losses resulting from changes and adjustments that might be denied initially. The divorcee who tries to maintain the same financial status finally realizes that she may need to sell her home or make other standard of living adjustments to survive financially. Children already struggling with the loss of a parent may additionally have to adjust to a new school, loss of friends, and a shared bedroom. Some divorced mothers will have to return to work to support their families. Divorced fathers may be forced to take on a second job to cover the expenses of two households. As a result of divorce, many children will lose their fathers' and mothers' consistent presence, guidance, and support in their home. These secondary losses may be more troublesome over time for the children than the primary loss of an absent parent.

One divorced woman said, "I had no idea there would be so many other changes and adjustments following my divorce. If I'd had to face it all at once, I would have never made it. Step by step, I have accepted my new life."

DEPRESSION

When you're depressed, you might say, "I feel like I'm in a big black hole. Nothing feels or looks good to me. I'm afraid I can't keep going."

Sadness is a normal reaction to a traumatic event and a common component of grief. It is different from depression. Depression can involve our thoughts, moods, and behaviors. When events seem beyond our control, the helplessness we feel can lead to depression. We may feel worried, overwhelmed, and anxious. Intense anxiety can lead to depression. We may feel empty, tearful, helpless, hopeless, worthless, and abandoned. We may move slowly or feel intense anger. Depression can also result from anger turned inward.

Some depressive symptoms can bring changes in our body's ability to function. We may see a change in weight, sleep, or appetite. We might not be able to perform as we used to at home, school, or work. If our situational depression persists, it can become a clinical depression (major depressive disorder), which means we'll likely need professional help or medication to recover.

One woman suffering from depression said, "I've lost my song." Another said, "The worse thing in life is to be alive . . . but dead inside."

Major depression involves not only changes in our ability to function, but it can actually lead us to a total inability to function. In extreme forms, individuals become incapacitated and are unable to care for themselves. Fortunately, even serious depression can be successfully treated by a professional. Major depressive disorders do not usually respond to the basic self-help tools alone (emoting, exercise, sunlight, diet, journaling). We may need psychotherapy and medications. Each year more than 11 million Americans suffer from serious depression. Of these, about 2 percent are children and 5 percent are adolescents.[2]

ANXIETY

Anxiety is a common symptom of loss and grief. Sometimes it is helpful to identify what is being threatened. It may be love, security, esteem, integrity, control, or success. During loss it is probably a combination of many.

Anxiety may appear in a variety of behaviors. One woman wrote: "As part of my grief work, I dove into overactivity. It seemed to be an attempt to validate my worth and redefine my purpose. I used my busyness and doing tasks in an attempt to find relief and a feeling of acceptance through my accomplishments. Through my overactivity, I was determined to make my life significant, meaningful, and productive in spite of my pain. All of this overactivity helped me cope as best I could. However, at first nothing seemed to make me feel better."

If we stay in overactive or avoidance modes for long periods of time, we may become stuck in the grief process, unable to totally resolve our issues. Research has shown that overdoing or overactivity can increase our anxiety and stress. We might take on more responsibility than we can realistically handle. Even small challenges can seem stressful during a crisis.

Many physical symptoms accompany anxiety. One mother writes about her anxiety after the loss of a baby: "My pulse raced, I couldn't breathe, sit still, or concentrate. I tried to do a hundred things at once. I got a lot of things done, but my anxiety never left me."

Another mother feeling vulnerable displays the same anxiety: "The other night the storm picked up so violently. I panicked and ran to find my three-year-old son. He is the only child I have left. I cannot bear another loss. I am angry I have these fears."

Job describes his anxiety as he faced his sufferings: "For the thing which I greatly feared is come upon me, and that which I was afraid of is come unto me. I was not in safety, neither had I rest, neither was I quiet; yet trouble came" (Job 3:25–26).

If anxiety persists or turns to panic attacks, professional help may be needed.

ANGER

Anger is a common emotion with any loss and can signal the beginning of acceptance. On the other hand, if your anger turns to rage, you should seek professional help, especially if there is danger of hurting yourself or someone else.

Women typically display less demonstrative anger than men. Society and likely biology have influenced women not to openly express their anger. Many will find ways to hold onto their anger. Anger repressed, ignored, shelved, or turned inward can lead to depression, confusion, guilt, or even physical illness. Some of us strike out at the very people we love. We may not be sure where to productively direct our anger.

Anger is usually a secondary emotion that can hide other deep emotions. A father who lost a child said to his wife, "When I act mean and angry, it just means I'm feeling sad and hurt inside."

Anger can also be a sign of unmet needs or expectations. Our assumptions of how our life should have been are lost. The loss of a safe, predictable world becomes a secondary loss. We may feel vulnerable and afraid of the future. Our anger can be a sign of healing, so we don't want to stuff it.

We may feel anger toward relatives, medical staff, and others for all the suffering we or our family has experienced. For a time we may feel life is meaningless. We might be angry at God for allowing us and our family to suffer. Even Job, whom God loved and accepted as righteous, expressed his anger toward God: "Let the day perish wherein I was born. . . . Why died I not from the womb? . . . Why is light given to a man whose way is hid, and whom God hath hedged in?" (Job 3:3, 11, 23). "I cry unto thee, and thou dost not hear me: I stand up and thou regardest me not. Thou art become cruel to me (Job 30:20–21).

Anger toward deity or leaders representing God following a crisis is common among all faiths. It can be more intense for the faithful who believed that God should have prevented their tragedy. We may become confused because we know that God is good and loves us, yet we wonder why our suffering continues. Experiencing feelings of anger toward God can produce guilt, which further complicates the grieving process. (See spiritual injury in chapter 3.) It can be overwhelming to face a serious loss while also experiencing a loss of faith or comfort from God.

GUILT

Guilt is another emotion that is common with any traumatic event or serious loss. For some people, this is the most exhausting and difficult emotion to deal with. According to B. Bush, "Guilt feelings are often a combination of many different feelings rather than one simple feeling . . . it's a messy mixture of insecurity, self-doubt, self-condemnation, self-judgment, anxiety, and fear."[3]

Following a traumatic experience, we often blame ourselves for not doing things differently to prevent the loss. A father writes: "If I had just noticed that something was wrong earlier and caught it sooner; I know I could have prevented this whole event."

A mother said: "I did so many things wrong. If I had just done things differently, this wouldn't have happened."

Another mother writes: "Since my child has died, I keep remembering how I got angry at him a few months before. What he did was really not his fault. I made him cry. He went to school late with red eyes. Even though I apologized when he got home, it hasn't erased the painful guilt from my memory."

Children experience guilt too: "If I hadn't wished my sister dead, she wouldn't be dying today." "If I had been a better boy, I wouldn't have gotten sick."

Guilt is a painful component of grief that manifests itself when we feel we should have been able to avert the tragedy that happened through our faith, prayers, or righteous living. We may ask ourselves, "What did I do wrong? Am I responsible for this event?" The guilt ridden words "I should have" may haunt us. It is an overwhelming burden for many to carry and endure.

Guilt was a strong emotion for Dennis and me following the death of our fourteen-year-old disabled son, Cameron. We felt responsible for his safety and care, and we experienced guilt when our decision to subject Cameron to surgery resulted in his early death.

We had been surprised by our doctor's advice. He informed us that Cameron's hips had deteriorated and he would need to have surgery within six months. I could see tears swelling up in Cameron's big brown eyes. I tried to reassure him. I told him that during the surgery he would be asleep and it wouldn't hurt and that when he woke up, he would get medication to keep him comfortable. The surgery could possibly remove his pain so he could ride his adapted tricycle better.

Dennis's guilt was intense. He was the one lying next to Cam when he died. He had kissed him good night shortly before and was relieved Cameron was resting so well with less pain. Had Cameron tried to call out to him? Should Dennis have noticed something was wrong? Had Cameron aspirated or choked, as one nurse and doctor thought, while his father slept next to him? Why didn't he hear something? The nurse was always in the room. Why hadn't she watched or listened closer?

How could Dennis ever let go of this painful blame and guilt? He sincerely felt that by falling asleep he had not protected Cameron. Neither our other children nor I could comfort him. He and Cam had showered, dressed, brushed teeth together, and often shared the same fork for fourteen years. The void and guilt he felt were beyond measure. He was a professional counselor and had helped others through their grief, yet he felt lost at first and unable to help himself.

We had both presented grief workshops and had experienced guilt before. We now realize we may have intellectually understood guilt; however, we hadn't emotionally felt or known this intense pain before. We had no idea that guilt could hurt so much and for so long.

We learned through this loss that there are no clear-cut answers for everyone on how to relieve guilt and pain. For us, talking about it and reframing it was helpful.

Cameron trusted the doctor's and our decision that surgery was best for him. In the 1992 movie *Robin Hood* with Kevin Costner, Robin had made what he thought was the best decision in behalf of his beloved and trusted blind friend, Duncan. He sent him away from the fighting and danger . . . only to find that he had been ruthlessly murdered anyway. Robin Hood felt enormous sorrow and guilt. Duncan was so perfect and obedient; Robin didn't feel he deserved to die. The guilt he felt for his decision was apparent and disabling. Then his mentor, the Great Azeem, seeing Robin's anguish counseled, "There are no perfect men, just perfect intentions." Most of us have "perfect intentions" for those we love. Sometimes beyond our control, something goes wrong. Even with the best plans, accidents happen and our loved ones can become ill or die.

It took a long time to work through our guilt, painful emotions, and questions; however, with time, work, and faith, we ultimately reconciled most of our grief.

Unresolved guilt is not healthy for any of us. If we do make a true mistake, we must remember that "to err is human."[4] None of us are perfect, and we all make mistakes. In fact, we may wish we had done something different. These guilt feelings need to be expressed and then hopefully we can let go and forgive ourselves.

One might also consider eliminating "shoulds" from their vocabulary. (If someone else shames you with too many "shoulds," you could respond back with, "Don't *should* on me!")

FALSE GUILT

In many instances, individuals are experiencing false guilt (blaming themselves for events and circumstances they are not really responsible for). They might say, "If I hadn't fallen asleep, I know I could have prevented his death."

After her child committed suicide, a parent asked, "Didn't I instill hope in my child?" This false guilt is a negative cognitive message that can delay recovery. False guilt can be resolved over time by integrating and expressing healthy and accurate thought processes and then by integrating them cognitively. A professional may need to assist you in this process.

CONTROL ISSUES

Many situations and circumstances in our lives are not controllable. The realization that we have little control over parts of our lives can make us feel vulnerable and afraid. To compensate for this fear, we may attempt to overcontrol others, especially those we may feel concern or responsible for.

A mother writes after her adversity: "I know I am driving my husband and children crazy. They claim I expect perfection from them. I become so frustrated when they don't do what I think they should. The need to control is an overpowering force since the death of my child. Some of it may be the vulnerability I feel. Like an overprotective instinct that something else bad might happen. I realize I am actually pushing the people away that I love the most. I feel the same frustration when someone tries to control me."

When we experience stress and frustration, we should ask ourselves, am I trying to control someone or something outside of my control, or is someone trying to overcontrol me?

LONGING, YEARNING, PINING, AND SEARCHING

For many, this stage of grief lasts the longest. We miss our loved one or our old life and how things use to be. Earth life may seem like a long time to wait before things improve or we see a deceased loved one again. We may have faith in the next life, but the spirit world seems far away right now. We may continue to ask, "Why me?" wishing to resolve questions that seem at first to have no satisfying answers. Even though we may have great faith and tap into the power of the gospel, we may still experience many of the painful symptoms associated with the grief process. Many of us will yearn for the way we thought things could or should be, and now may never be. We search for answers, yearning for hope or peace to return to our lives. We start to wonder if we will ever feel any better. We might conclude that we must be going crazy or doing something wrong to still be in so much pain. These feelings can be very confusing. The fear of something else going wrong hangs over us. Everyone thinks you are better, and you hate to admit you're not. You find it hard to believe that it may take eighteen to twenty-four months[5] to find relief, and then depending on the loss, additional years to achieve a functioning recovery.

HURT AND CONFUSION

Your friends, relatives, ward members, and coworkers may feel uncomfortable around you. They may seem to ignore you because of their awkwardness. They may not understand the intensity and duration of your grief or may feel helpless to console and comfort you. Consequently, many offer clichés or platitudes in an attempt to heal you. These sayings often bring hurt and confusion even though they are offered by people who sincerely want to help. Because others have not had your experiences, it is difficult for them to understand the depth and length of your grief.

BARGAINING

Bargaining during adversity is common. We may make promises to ourselves, others, or God. In return we seek acceptance, answers to our prayers, improved health, or some other miracle.

DISORIENTATION AND DISORGANIZATION

Any traumatic event can cause confusion, disorientation, and disorganization in our lives. The intense reactions can cause a lack of concentration or absent-mindedness.

WITHDRAWAL, ISOLATION, AND LONELINESS

When we feel no one can understand or respond to our pain, it is common to withdraw from community, church, friends, and family. However, it becomes unhealthy if isolation becomes a permanent solution to our mourning.

We may isolate ourselves to the point of no return. We may refuse help and stop reaching out to others. We stop sharing our concerns and feelings. Soon we find no one calls or comes around. This self-imposed isolation may feel safer initially. Yet, with time, we may become lonely and bitter, unable to function and find healing. We might lose our ability to feel joy, interact with, or help others.

Ultimate loneliness may occur when we feel separated and misunderstood not only by others, but by God. (See spiritual injury in chapter 3.)

Physical Effects Resulting from Stress and Loss

The list of physical symptoms is extensive. We may feel physical pain or aching as the shock and numbness wear off. We may experience a tightness or hollowness in our stomach or chest, breathing difficulties, or a dry mouth. Our heart may pound so fast and hard that we feel we could surely die, or wish we would! We may be restless, unable to sit still, or so weak and exhausted we cannot possibly move. Many people experience changes in bowel, appetite, and sleep patterns. Some experience headaches, blurred vision, and nervous twitches. The immune system is often suppressed with grief and stress. Individuals experiencing a traumatic situation have a higher incidence of physical illness and death, up to two years following their loss.[6] Physical symptoms may also be intensified by emotional reactions, such as guilt, depression, anger, anxiety, resentment, or bitterness. The majority of individuals seeking medical help or hospitalization have in their recent history experienced a major loss.

Intellectual/Cognitive Processing Following a Loss

Grief affects us cognitively through our thoughts. It includes the process that we experience as we attempt to comprehend or understand what has happened to us. We may repeatedly ask the same questions. We may be trying to intellectually make sense out of what has occurred. Through this mental rumination we sift through each bit of information in an attempt to intellectually assimilate, grasp, or understand the events. This mental repetition is often an attempt to substitute different solutions that would have altered our outcome. We may think, "What if I had done this?" or "What if we had gone there?" We mentally search for a way that we could have a different or better conclusion, diagnosis, or prognosis. It can become very frightening as the mind tries to regain some control by recreating or replaying parts of the experience. These repeated thought processes may eventually help us accept what has happened. We will have to make cognitive adjustments to process this new information.

We may feel irritable with noise or other stimulation, as it is difficult to concentrate on anything except what has happened to us. This preoccupation may cloud our brain and limit our ability to function at previous levels of competency and for extended periods of time.

We may also try to intellectualize the details of our loss without allowing for feelings or emotions. When we are ready to do our grief work, we may need help transferring this knowledge from our heads to our hearts so we can experience greater congruency with our emotions. As A. D. Wolfelt puts it, we may need to "feel it to heal it."[7]

It may take weeks, months, or even years to sort it all out. However, with time, we slowly begin to comprehend what has happened and what it means for our future.

How Men and Women Process Grief

Men and women grieve in the intellectual and emotional dimensions differently. The majority of women are right-brain dominant, meaning they function more from the brain's right hemisphere, which is associated with feelings and emotions. Many men, on the other hand, are left-brain dominant and are more likely to be governed by logic and reasoning. Women are often better at emotionally expressing grief than men. Men usually do better sorting out the intellectual details of their loss. Both men and women do best when they utilize an appropriate balance of cognitive reasoning, while allowing themselves to emote.

Grief is felt inside; mourning is the outward manifestation of grief. Men often grieve inwardly, not displaying the outward signs of mourning. Some may express themselves through tears, while others are very quiet and stoic. Others busily start planning and doing many tasks.

The Social/Behavioral Process During Loss

During a crisis, we often experience grief symptoms that will effect our social interactions. Adversity affects our behaviors and how we function at work, home, church, and in other social settings. In the beginning we may feel uncomfortable around others and at social events, causing additional or secondary losses. Because our church membership represents a way of life within

our community, the social interactions among close church asso-
ciates has a greater potential to help or hurt our healing.

We may isolate ourselves from friends, family, and church
members. We try to protect ourselves from the constant reminder
of what others still have and we have lost. We might feel shame
and embarrassment, especially if we are not living up to our own
expectations or the expectations of those around us. We may
force ourselves to appear strong, acting as though we are healing
rapidly. We might not feel comfortable sharing the details of our
painful emotions and circumstances. We fear that others will not
understand our pain, or will judge us harshly. We may feel vulnerable and fear that more loss will occur in the future. These social
challenges are often damaging to our self-esteem.

Identity/Self-esteem

Our identity includes personal characteristics, body image,
talents, and disabilities. Many of our perceptions are learned as
we interact with our environment and others. When there are
changes in our physical body or environment, we have to make
emotional, behavioral, and mental adjustments. This may include
viewing ourselves differently.

During trials and adversity, we may also experience a loss of
identity and feel as if part of us has died. One sufferer writes:
"After my crisis, I think I lost some of my self-esteem. I tried to
feel I was still useful and valuable. I felt that others at church

expected me to move on as if nothing had happened. I tried to do this in a variety of ways. However, I felt lost for a long time."

We may lose our confidence, feeling that others are judging us as inadequate, which leaves us feeling vulnerable and afraid.

Abuse and other destructive experiences may cause us to feel unaccepted. We then turn to pleasing behaviors that we hope will secure us the love and attention we need. Many professionals call these pleasing behaviors masks or facades because we don't accurately portray our true self.[8] We may appear emotionally healthy, yet on the inside we are confused, lonely, anxious, or depressed. *Identity crisis* is another term used to describe this loss of self-esteem.

We may have to confront past pains that have been hidden away. Honestly acknowledging the hurt and pain is often an important step as we begin our healing. It may be helpful to relive and reclaim past behaviors, qualities, or feelings in a safe environment with a competent gospel-centered psychotherapist. If we repress or suppress grief, we may experience a similar loss of self. We try to hurry and get through our pain and pretend to carry on as usual. Some encourage our denial by complimenting us on how strong we are or how much faith we must have to recover so quickly. We then continue to project this false self in an attempt to save face and look as strong and healthy as we perceive others believe and want us to be.

Caregivers who give so much of themselves to another for an extended time may feel part of their own identity or self-image is lost at the death of the person for whom they are caring. This void can be enormous and adds a unique dimension to their grief. This is true of any worthwhile endeavor or any person who has occupied much of our time, thought, or worries for months or years.

One caretaker writes, "After caring for him for so many years, I wondered, what will I do now? Where do I turn? As I tried to regain or redefine my identity, it seemed more than I could endure at times."

Disenfranchised Grief

People experience disenfranchised grief when they incur a loss that is not or cannot be openly acknowledged, publicly mourned, or socially supported.[9] For example, one of our associate's husbands had divorced her and also abandoned much support of their children. He died soon after their divorce, and she and the children stood at the casket. They were not really mourning his death since their grief had taken place much earlier during the divorce. However, in the shadows, in the back of the room, was a grieving woman. She had hoped to marry him the following month. Her grief was disenfranchised because no one acknowledged or accepted her sorrow.

I felt a twinge of disenfranchised grief last week at my daughter's wedding, which was three and a half weeks after my mother's death. I had worked hard to make it a happy, picture-perfect day, which it turned out to be. No one really mentioned that my mother wasn't there. At one point when the grandparents were taking pictures with the bride and groom, I wanted to shout out, "Ashley's grandma would be here in the pictures and supporting us all, but she died three weeks ago!"

Complicated or Prolonged Grief

Somewhere between 10 and 20 percent of those mourning a serious loss will experience prolonged or complicated grief. Grief may become complicated for a variety of reasons. Common situations resulting in a complicated bereavement include (1) a loss that is preventable or the family member feels responsible for the illness or death of their loved one; (2) a loss resulting from suicide or murder; (3) the loss of children; (4) if someone's illness, death, or suffering is prolonged; (5) when the loss conflicts with spiritual expectations; and (6) multiple losses or deaths. Any one or a combination of the above complications can increase the duration and intensity of our grief.

Adjusting and adapting to significant loss can take many months or years. It may be appropriate and helpful to refer families or individuals for psychotherapy and medication support at any time if you see any of the following symptoms: (1) refusing social support; (2) chronic or persistent depression; (3) failure to provided needed self-care; (4) persistent thoughts of suicide; (5) addictions; (6) history of mental illness; (7) lack of trust; (8) excessive anger or rage; (9) excessive anxiety or panic attacks; and (10) inability to plan one's future and move forward.

Complicated grief symptoms form the following cluster, which is distinct from depression and anxiety symptom clusters:

- Intense yearning and heartache
- Guilt about moving on
- Lack of acceptance
- Lack of trust
- Excessive anger or bitterness
- Numbness and detachment
- Inability to move forward
- Feeling that life is empty and meaningless
- Lack of hope for future happiness
- Irritability and agitation[10]

A diagnosis of complicated mourning using the above symptoms would generally not apply until six months following the loss. Complicated mourning increases the risk for suicidal thoughts and behaviors, cardiac events, high blood pressure, cancer, and other physical symptoms.

Professional support and assistance will be helpful for individuals and families grieving and is especially beneficial for those experiencing complicated or chronic bereavement.

Harold B. Lee said, "Members may need counseling more than clothing and members who, through bishops, are referred to an agency in our [family] social services program should feel no more hesitancy in asking for help of this kind than we should in requesting help through the priesthood welfare program."[11]

Even with intense or complicated grief, we can adjust, adapt, and reconcile our loss. Human beings are highly resilient to loss and trauma. We can help ourselves by acknowledging our loss and grief and finding meaning in our sadness or suffering. Facing loss and finding personal meaning will enable us to identify hope for a positive future.

Notes

1. Rana K. Limbo and Sara Rich Wheeler, *When a Baby Dies: A Handbook for Helping and Healing* (La Crosse Lutheran Hospital/Gunderson Clinic, Ltd., 1986), xiv.
2. Michael D. Yapko, *Hand-Me-Down Blues* (New York: Golden Books, 1999), 8.
3. B. Bush, *Guilt—A Tool for Christian Growth* (St. Meinrad, Indiana: Abbey Press, 1991).
4. C. Thurman, *These Truths We Must Believe* (Nashville: Thomas Nelsen, 1991), 23.
5. Glen W. Davidson, *Understanding Mourning* (Minneapolis: Augsburg Publishing House, 1984).
6. Ibid.
7. A. D. Wolfelt, "Lessons in Caregiving for the Dying," workshop handout, Dallas Market Center, Aug. 22, 1996.
8. Joan Borysenko, *Minding the Body, Mending the Mind* (Reading, Massachusetts: Addison-Wesley, 1987), 57.
9. J. K. Doka, ed. *Disenfranchised Grief: Recognizing Hidden Sorrow* (Lexington, Massachusetts: Lexington Books, 1989), 3–7.
10. *Bereavement Care Journal*, Winter 2004, vol. 23 no. 3, 3–7.
11. Harold B. Lee, Seminar for Regional Representatives of the Twelve, Oct. 1, 1970.

CHAPTER THREE

Spiritual Hurt and Healing

ONE OF THE MOST HURTFUL ASPECTS OF coping with loss and adversity is that it can impact us spiritually. Spiritual injury results when life experiences contradict our previously held spiritual assumptions. Spiritual pain can occur when someone feels abandoned or forsaken by God. Some plead for a miracle healing, realizing in the end that they must ultimately adjust, suffer, endure, and even die.

How can we prevent the negative events that happen to us from having a negative impact on us? It may be helpful to remember that painful trials and tribulations are part of our earth life experience. Church leaders and latter-day scripture suggest we agreed or were made aware that trials would accompany our mortal existence. New Testament scripture also promises comfort for those suffering in a future estate: "The sufferings of this present time are not worthy to be compared with the glory which shall be revealed in us" (Romans 8:18).

Many bereaved members of the Church indicate that their first step in healing from spiritual injury occurred when they felt safe enough to honestly and openly express their fear, anger, and doubt. A mother whose daughter died of cancer said, "I may not know what I believe about God any longer." The following insight, love, and acceptance expressed by her church leader helped her through the healing process: "God can handle your anger, fear, and doubt. You are not the only person to ever question your beliefs during a tragedy."

What a relief for this woman experiencing spiritual injury to find someone willing to listen and accept her confusion and pain without condemning judgment. She was then able to start the process of spiritual healing and forgiveness. With unconditional love and support, many can begin to nourish their faith again by returning to prayer, scripture reading, and church attendance. Most grieving individuals heal and return to their faith with sufficient time, support, and grief work.

An active wife and mother reluctantly shares her spiritual injury: "After my loss, I had to start all over again with my testimony and beliefs. At first I was so hurt that God had not prevented my tragedy that I couldn't read LDS doctrine or much from the Book of Mormon. I wanted to learn what others believed. Slowly my spiritual pain improved and I returned to my own faith, doctrines, and a love for the Book of Mormon."

A grieving, committed member shares her anger toward God: "If I didn't believe in God, I wouldn't be angry at him now for not protecting me from this tragedy."[1]

Belief in God also allows us to feel His power and comfort. Some who ask, "Where is God?" in their personal crisis may over time benefit from opening their heart again to truly find His love. After expressing confusion and anger, many will be able to let go of their fears and look with reassurance and hope again to Him.

Faith and Grief Co-exist

After our son Cameron's death, we were confused at first because we hoped that if we had enough faith we wouldn't hurt. We hoped that we would be shielded from the painful feelings of grief. We came to realize that faith and grief can co-exist. Knowing Cameron still existed in the spirit world was very comforting, but that didn't stop us from missing him here and now.

As Dennis and I have worked with other grieving individuals, we have discovered many deeply faithful Church members who wonder why they were feeling such profound pain when they had been obedient and faithful. Some have been hurt or confused when they were referred to 1 Corinthians 10:13: "God is faithful, who will not suffer you to be tempted above that ye are able; but will with the temptation also make a way to escape, that ye may be able to bear it." In

Alma 13:28–29 we are cautioned to watch and pray "that ye may not be tempted above that which ye can bear."

These scriptures use the word *tempted*, which may have a different connotation than physical or emotional suffering. The phrase "tempted more than we have strength to resist" may have more to do with sin than adversity, pain, and grief. Dennis and I have met many who feel they are not guilty of sin, yet acknowledge they are barely hanging on as they face adverse circumstances and suffering. If individuals do give in to temptation and sin, it is generally not our place to judge whether they had the emotional or mental strength to resist their personal temptations. Only God knows what their current mental, physical, and spiritual strengths and weaknesses are. It is often more helpful to recognize and understand that exercising faith and obedience does not preclude individuals from experiencing grief.

Mourning for our loss does not mean that we are weak or that we have lost our faith. Grieving, crying, and feeling pain for our situation is not evidence that we don't have sufficient faith or are weak. We can believe in God, life after death, and all the truths of the gospel and still experience profound pain, grief, and sadness in our mortal life.

During the grief process, it is also common to question God and some of our previous beliefs. Some have embraced false interpretations of doctrine that should be altered and reframed. This is especially difficult if these false beliefs or traditions were ingrained through reinforcement by our parents or other significant individuals. The following scriptures discuss how the traditions of our fathers influence us: Mosiah 1:5, Matthew 7:8, Alma 3:8, and Alma 9:16.

A confused member of the Church experiencing a significant trial stated: "My mother taught me I would be protected and blessed if I lived the gospel. I interpreted this to mean, because I was a good person living all the commandments, this tragedy would never happen to me."

It is helpful to understand that being protected and blessed doesn't necessarily mean being exempt from trials. It does mean we can receive direction and be strengthened to endure our trials in ways similar to Christ, Joseph Smith, and other prophets. It might be well to remind ourselves that we will "receive no witness until after the trial of [our] faith" (Ether 12:6).

Attempting to console those who have lost loved ones or endured serious trials by saying, "It will be better in the next life," tends to minimize their immediate pain. "It's like you're on a desert and you are dying of thirst, and someone says, 'Yes, you can have a drink, but not for thirty years!' "[2] Yes, we will see our loved one again or be relieved from our adversity in the next life. However, that ultimate destination for many follows a long and at times very painful earthly journey!

Elder M. Russell Ballard said,

> Life isn't always easy. At some point in our journey we may
> feel much as the pioneers did as they crossed Iowa—up to our

knees in mud, forced to bury some of our dreams along the way. We all face rocky ridges, with the wind in our face and winter coming on too soon. Sometimes it seems as though there is no end to the dust that stings our eyes and clouds our vision. Sharp edges of despair and discouragement jut out of the terrain to slow our passage. . . . Occasionally we reach the top of one summit in life, as the pioneers did, only to see more mountain peaks ahead, higher and more challenging than the one we have just traversed. Tapping unseen reservoirs of faith and endurance, we, as did our forebears, inch ever forward toward that day when our voices can join with those of all pioneers who have endured in faith, singing, "All is well! All is well!"[3]

God Provides Miracles and Allows Agency

It is healing for us to believe that God can and does intervene in our lives and that miracles do happen. The scriptures teach us that "God has not ceased to be a God of miracles" (Mormon 9:15) and miracles have not ceased (Moroni 7:27–29; Mormon 9:19).

It can be equally healing to understand that in most instances, God allows natural laws and consequences to run their course. Many will have to endure earth life experiencing significant illness, disabilities, or other loss and emotional pain. Our miracle or healing may not occur in this life, and our faith will be tried (3 Nephi 26:11).

Often we refer to miracles as guaranteed, predictable events when they are, in reality, hoped for examples of how God can work in our lives. Following the shooting at Columbine High

School, the bombing of the Oklahoma Federal Building, the September 11 terrorist attack, and the Salt Lake City Trolley Square shooting, many questioned why some victims survived and others did not. Some of those interviewed said, "I am grateful that God protected and spared my life and the life of my loved one." Consider the unsaid message conveyed to those who lost loved ones. This may sound harsh; however, what many victims heard was, "God did not protect my loved one," or "We were not worthy of His protection."

The same unsaid messages often apply to other kinds of loss and adversity. Bereavement counselors who interviewed individuals following the Oklahoma City bombing concluded that those who were coping best believed God did not cause or intend this horrible event and that God was, in fact, grieving with them. Those who were not coping as well believed that God controls and orchestrates all events and thus was responsible for the bombing and the deaths of their loved ones.

Many have asked, "Why does God allow good, innocent men, women, and children to suffer?" If their suffering is caused by someone else, it is helpful to explain that God permits individual agency. God allows choice (Alma 60:13). Evil individuals can hurt and even murder other innocent victims who are living gospel-centered lives. Moral agency is an important doctrine and principle of the gospel. It was Satan's plan to destroy our agency. With our agency, we are free to make good or poor choices. Alma and Amulek watched as faithful believers were burned. Amulek was tempted to use God's power to save them. However, Alma restrained him and said, "The spirit constraineth me. . . . The Lord . . . doth suffer that . . . people may do this thing . . . that the judgments which he shall exercise upon them in his wrath may be just; and the blood of the innocent shall stand as a witness against them" (Alma 14:11).

Moroni taught that in some circumstances the Lord permits the righteous to suffer or even die as a result of another's sinful use of agency so that "His justice and judgment may come upon the wicked" (Alma 60:13).

At times Dennis and I have felt we had witnessed miracles. At other times we felt that we really needed a miracle and it seemed to be withheld. We witnessed miracles in our oldest son Darren's illness. We also experienced times when the promised blessings didn't seem to come in the way we had hoped for. He endured lengthy physical suffering, emotional despair, and spiritual disappointments. Understanding the reasons seven surgeries weren't successful was difficult, but we went forward with hope that the total healing promised through blessings would eventually come. Sometimes we felt as Job did, that no one could understand our suffering. On two different occasions we were told by well meaning friends and relatives, "Will you just tell Darren to learn what he is supposed to learn so he can get better?" The unsaid message came through loud and clear: "Your son's medical illness is caused by God. It results from Darren not knowing something he must learn through his suffering." Clichés and unkind words from individuals that cause spiritual injury or "enlarge the wounds of those already wounded" do not flow from God, Christ, or the Holy Ghost (Jacob 2:9). Two years and eight surgeries later, Darren was finally completely healed.

God Has Given Us the Comforter

We are less likely to become overwhelmed if we can focus on God as our source and author of all spiritual tools. He gave us the Atonement through His Son and the companionship of the Holy Ghost as His voice. The scriptures testify that Jesus Christ understands our grief: Christ is a "man of sorrows, and acquainted with grief" (Isaiah 53:3). The Holy Ghost is a comforter and the revealer of truth. All insights and reassurances that can bring spiritual healing originate from Godly sources.

God is always there to comfort and support us through our trials: "I will not leave you comfortless. I will come to you" (John 14:18). "Look unto God with firmness of mind, and pray unto him with exceeding faith, and he will console you in your afflictions, and he will plead your cause" (Jacob 3:1).

"He hath sent me to bind up the broken hearted . . . to comfort all that mourn; to appoint unto them that mourn in Zion, to give unto them beauty for ashes, the oil of joy for mourning, the garment of praise for the spirit of heaviness" (Isaiah 61:1–3). God hears us in our affliction (Alma 33:11). "And God will wipe away all tears from their eyes" (Revelation 21:4).

Although we may not understand why some people are healed and others are not, it is comforting to know God does have the ultimate power to heal us physically, mentally, and spiritually. Alma taught that "He will take upon him . . . the sicknesses of his people" (Alma 7:11) and He will succor us in our weaknesses (Alma 7:12).

There Is a Balance with Justice and Mercy

President John Taylor taught, "There may be circumstances arise in this world to pervert for a season the order of God, to change the designs of the Most High, apparently, for the time being. Yet they will ultimately roll back into their proper place—Justice will have its place, and so will Mercy, and every man and woman will yet stand in their true position before God."[4]

Mortal life can seem endless for those facing long-term adversity. Earth life is not necessarily fair. According to Neal A. Maxwell, "If it's fair, it is not a true trial."[5]

It can be helpful for innocent victims to know that God is just and merciful and that there will be justice for those who use their agency inappropriately. The principle of God punishing the wicked is taught throughout the scriptures: "The wages of sin are death" (Romans 6:23). Spiritual death results in a separation from God. The Lord will judge and punish the unjust (Deuteronomy 24:16; 2 Peter 2:4; Mormon 4:5; Alma 42:22).

Why Me? Why Now? Why This Way?

The following letter was written by a mother to her teenage son who was killed in a bike/truck accident. It displays the common confusion and questions when adversity strikes: "I love you so. I'm so sorry that I wasn't there that morning, to not let you ride, for not making you go with me that terrible day. I love you so much. All I want for you is to be happy. Please, please be happy. Please be with us in Eternal Life. Was this the way it was supposed to be?"[6]

The *whys* are a common and painful part of adversity. We think we have finally resolved them, and then we ask again. There seems to be different kinds of *whys*: "Why did this happen, God? Why did this happen logically or medically?" Dennis and I asked those questions. We wanted to know the details of what happened when Cam's heart stopped, why Darren's surgeries failed, and when another son would overcome his struggle with addictions.

The irony of our *whys* is this question: "How often in happy times did you ask, why?"[7] Many have found, "He who has a Why to live for can endure almost any How."[8]

Elder Neal A. Maxwell explains that trials come to us from three general categories:[9]

Type 1: *Trials we bring on ourselves by the sinful choices and mistakes we make.* Some blame God for trials resulting from our personal choices and overly identify with Job, when in actuality our trial is self-imposed. A scriptural example of the consequences of a sinful choice is found in the story of King David. David made a series of choices that ultimately resulted in an act of adultery with Bathsheba and the death of her husband, Uriah (2 Samuel 11:2).

Type 2: *Trials that are part of earth life.* For example, people get sick, have accidents, endure old age, and die. We could also add to this category those who suffer innocently from the sinful choices of others—those abused, murdered, and betrayed. Most of the suffering we experience here is a product of the vulnerabilities and realities of earth life, including the misuse of agency by others. The Lord doesn't fly airplanes into international trade centers or drive the car of the alcoholic who takes the life of an innocent child playing in his path. Nor does God, in most instances, though He could, prevent these events from occurring.

Type 3: *Trials God uses to refine us.* "But he knoweth the way that I take: when he hath tried me, I shall come forth as gold" (Job 23:10). When Christ was asked if a man's blindness was the result of sin, He answered: "Neither hath this man sinned, nor his parents: but that the works of God should be made manifest in him" (John 9:3).

Dennis's and my personal experiences and observations over years of counseling have caused us to conclude that the vast majority of the challenges and suffering we face on this earth are Type 2 suffering, resulting from the realities and trials of earth life.

Elder Maxwell further stated, "The sudden loss of health, wealth, self-esteem, status, or a loved one—developments that may stun us—are foreseen by God, though not necessarily caused by him."[10]

It is not our place to decide which of the three types of adversity our neighbors are experiencing. Our tendency to judge others more critically than ourselves is humorously illustrated in the following definitions:

- **Punishing:** what the Lord is doing to your Gentile neighbor when misfortunes come.
- **Chastening:** what the Lord is doing to your LDS neighbor when adversity hits.
- **Testing:** what the Lord is doing when a bad thing happens to you.

When he was a member of the Quorum of the Twelve, Spencer W. Kimball authored a pamphlet called *Tragedy or Destiny*. He humbly cautions that the pamphlet contains many of his own thoughts and personal beliefs. Nevertheless, Elder Kimball's personal revelation is insightful and poses some challenging questions for each of us to ponder. He asks, "Does the Lord cause tragedies in people's lives?" and "Why does the Lord let these terrible things happen?" A child drowned, several people were killed in a plane crash, and a young elder was killed in the mission field. Elder Kimball asks, "Was it the Lord who directed the plane to crash or the drowning to occur?" He raises the question, "Could the Lord have prevented these tragedies?" He confirms that the answer is definitely yes. The Lord is omnipotent with all power. However, Elder

Kimball poses additional questions: What if the Lord always punished the wicked and blessed the righteous? How would the gospel law of moral agency work? Wouldn't we always choose righteousness if we were immediately blessed? Wouldn't the wicked choose righteousness if they were immediately punished? Would they continue to choose to be wicked? Should the righteous be protected from hardship, pain, suffering, sacrifice, or tragedy?

Elder Kimball concluded:

> But if all the sick were healed, if all the righteous were protected and the wicked destroyed, the whole program of the Father would be annulled and the basic principal of the gospel, free agency, would be ended. If pain and sorrow and total punishment immediately followed the doing of evil, no soul would repeat a misdeed. If joy and peace and rewards were instantaneously given to the doer of good, there would be no evil—all would do good and not because of the rightness of doing good, there would be no test of strength, no development of character, no growth of powers, no free agency, only satanic controls. Should all prayers be immediately answered according to our selfish desires and our limited understanding, then there would be little or no suffering, sorrow, disappointment or even death, and if these were not there would also be an absence of joy, success, resurrection, eternal life and Godhood.[11]

Would God have protected Paul from his "thorn in the flesh" (2 Corinthians 12:7)? The Lord said unto him, "My grace is sufficient for thee: for my strength is made perfect in weakness. Most gladly therefore will I rather glory in my infirmities that the power of Christ may rest upon me" (2 Corinthians 12:9).

Would we have allowed Jesus to stay on the cross? Would we have allowed the Prophet Joseph Smith to suffer in Liberty Jail, and later die in the Carthage Jail if we had all power?

Sometimes when we ask *why*, we are really saying, "Lord, let me be in control, give me the reigns, everything will work out better if I'm in control. I doubt God's goodness because He does not use His power exactly as I wish."[12]

Orson F. Whitney taught: "No pain that we suffer, no trial that we experience is wasted. It ministers to our education, to the development of such qualities as patience, faith, fortitude and humility. All that we suffer and all that we endure, especially when we endure it patiently, builds up our character, purifies our hearts, expands our souls, and makes us more tender and charitable, more worthy to be called the children of God."[13]

Is It God's Will?

One mother asked, "Was it God's will that my daughter was raped and murdered?" Many hurting members of the Church have struggled when they were told their adversity is God's will. It seems helpful when we say something like this to them: "It is certainly God's will that we experience earth life and return to Him. God created this world where we experience pain, sickness, accidents, and death." "However, to say to the suffering individual that God's finger was on the trigger or that he caused someone to be murdered, raped, abused or betrayed is a cruel and unreasonable false doctrine."[14]

Am I Being Punished?

Some fear their tragedy is a punishment for past sins. Belated confessions to extramarital affairs, Church inactivity, breaking commandments, and dishonesty are common when personal tragedy occurs. These shortcomings often come quickly to mind when life's circumstances seem out of our control. When we receive blessings from God, it is through obedience to eternal laws (D&C 130:20–21). Conversely, some of us may inevitably reason that when we don't receive blessings or protection from God, it is always a result of our personal weakness and sin. After a crisis, these and other perceived truisms quickly flood our minds, complicating our grieving. We may search for some wrong we did in the past to explain our present loss. The association of loss and shortcomings may actually increase the complexity of our grief process. However, if our adversity is indeed a result of sin, then it is important that we utilize repentance as a healing tool.

As we confront adversity, we must evaluate each situation and when appropriate eliminate incorrect and erroneous thinking.

A grieving father experiencing multiple losses asks, "Would God punish or teach me by causing my daughter to experience abuse, my wife to get cancer, or my child to die, or does he allow these events and provide the resources and support necessary for our personalized growth and development toward Godhood?"[15]

The Prophet Joseph Smith taught, "It is an unhallowed principle to say that such and such have transgressed because they have been preyed upon by disease or death, for all flesh is subject to death and the Savior has said, 'judge not' lest 'ye be judged.' "[16]

If we accept that living the best we can inevitably falls short of all that is ultimately required, we will question less that we are responsible for all of life's disappointments and tragedies that come our way.

Elder Merrill J. Bateman, an emeritus member of the Quorum of the Seventy, said, "When one understands that trials are not necessarily the result of one's own doing, the test may be easier to endure."[17]

Refining

We should be hesitant in telling someone else that God is refining them as He refined Job. "I will refine them as silver is refined, and will try them as gold is tried" (Zechariah 13:11).

Examples in scripture of how God uses trials and affliction in specific instances may not be a representative sampling of how most of our life's trials originate. "Nevertheless the Lord seeth fit to chasten his people; yea, he trieth their patience and their faith" (Mosiah 23:21).

Elder Neal Maxwell explains that "there may be those who choose to debate . . . whether . . . God gives us a particular trial or simply declines to remove it."[18] If we can be patient and endure, the Lord can consecrate our afflictions (2 Nephi 2:2) and support us in our trials (Alma 36:3).

Am I Being Tested?

Some have also answered their "why me" questions by concluding that God is testing them, trying to see what they are made of. The previous conclusions could apply. Certainly we believe that all life has meaning and purpose and is a test. But should we look to God for inflicting every challenge or thorny problem directly on us as an assignment from Him, or are most of our trials a result of living in a world where adversity exists?

Some members of the Church are offended when they are told during a crisis that God is trying to tell them or teach them something. God certainly does allow us to learn and grow through adversity. However, making God responsible for divorce, accidents, or illness may result in serious spiritual injury.

A spiritual nonmember client in her late twenties was sure that the two miscarriages following her marriage were a direct punishment from God. She reasoned that because she had an abortion as a sixteen-year-old, she needed chastisement. She also carried a lot of guilt because she had never told her parents about the abortion. The repentance process proved healing for her, and she eventually did have a healthy full-term baby. However, the question remained, was her miscarriage inflicted on her because of her sin, or had the abortion she chose caused physical damage to her body that resulted in her compromised ability to maintain a full-term pregnancy?

Repentance and the Atonement

The previously mentioned client's crisis did, fortunately, encourage her to go through the repentance process and experience God's forgiveness. In John we are told if we confess our sins, God will forgive (1 John 1:9). If we don't repent, God is slow to answer our prayers and deliver us from afflictions (Mosiah 11:23–25). Through the Atonement we can be turned into another man and receive a new heart (1 Samuel 10:6, 9). "Faith and repentance bringeth a change of heart" (Helaman 15:7).

Elder Boyd K. Packer gives a beautiful parable of the Atonement, repentance, justice, and mercy. He tells of a man who wanted more material things than he could afford to buy. He promised his creditor that he would work hard and pay his debt off slowly with time. However, when the deadline came, the debtor was lacking and could not pay. The creditor put chains on his hands and feet and was ready to send him off to prison. As the debtor was crying and mourning the justice of his fate, a compassionate friend stepped forward, offering the debtor mercy by paying his debt. The chains were removed and the debtor was told he was free to go. With gratitude he agreed to finish paying his debt to this new creditor who had shown him mercy. This allegory teaches us that in spite of all we do, we are all lacking and come up short until Christ steps in to pay our debt with His Atonement as we repent.

Christ suffered "the pains of every living creature, both men, women, and children" (2 Nephi 9:21). This suffering is not just limited to sin, "but also the cumulative burden of all depression, all loneliness, all sorrow."[19]

The Savior has felt the pain and suffering brought about by living single, losing loved ones, facing illness, and enduring disabilities. He knows the pain and disappointment following a difficult divorce. He is no stranger to life's many losses. He willingly bears all these burdens and as our personal Savior understands our every suffering. Isaiah taught, "In all their affliction, he was afflicted, and the angel of his presence saved them: in his love and in his pity . . . he redeemed them, and carried them" (Isaiah 63:9).

Elder David A. Bednar said, "The enabling power of the Atonement strengthens us to do and be good and serve beyond our own individual desire and natural capacity."[20]

Forgiveness

"Forgiveness can increase emotional and physical healing. Being unwilling to forgive can 'FREEZE' you."[21]

Forgiveness can be part of our spiritual healing. However, it may take time and a lot of spiritual grief work to accomplish such a task. How do you forgive someone who has hurt you? Acts of betrayal may be especially painful.

Many have asked, "Can I forgive a perpetrator if they have not repented? Can I forgive without hearing the words 'I'm sorry'?"

"The reality of the situation is that no amount of talking, no analysis of why the betrayal occurred will completely do away with the hurt. No penalty can be handed down that will satisfactorily pay off the debt. No matter how cruelly you've been treated, the power to forgive does not lie within the person who hurt you . . . the blocks to forgiveness are ultimately within you. Forgiveness can stop the cycle of hurt."[22]

As we hope for God's forgiveness through the Atonement, we must also offer forgiveness to others and ourselves. Many of our struggles originate from someone who has hurt us. It is important to remember that Christ has assumed the unpaid balance of wrongdoings and imperfections incurred by those who have hurt us. We can find peace by allowing Christ to intervene and by letting go of our pain. As difficult as it may seem, we no longer need to focus on others' sins. This letting go is not only for them but, more important, for us.

The following false beliefs and biases can limit our ability to forgive someone who has hurt, abused, or betrayed us:

1. Forgiving allows perpetrators to get away with something.
2. Forgiveness is a sign of personal weakness.
3. Forgiving will cause the abuse to occur again.
4. Not forgiving helps punish the perpetrator.

5. The perpetrator must repent or apologize before I can forgive.

Forgiving someone is difficult, but it is possible. One woman said, "My spouse has been unfaithful. After our divorce he remarried and divorced again. We have now decided to try and to put our temple marriage back together. It's been so hard to trust and forgive. However, I feel I need to try."[23]

How do you forgive the man who robbed, raped, or murdered your loved one? One parent said, "My daughter was raped and murdered. It has been seven years. I will never forget or get over it. However, I am trying to forgive."[24]

Only through the power of Christ and the Atonement can one heal from such trauma. The Lord commanded: "Ye ought to forgive one another; . . . it is required to forgive *all* men" (D&C 64:9–10; Matthew 18:35; emphasis added).

The following tools have proven helpful to those attempting to offer forgiveness:

1. Write a letter to the offender; the letter may or may not be mailed.
2. Keep a journal of your feelings and memories, which may be personal or shared with trusted others.
3. Visualize and confront the offender (in an empty chair or through guided imagery with a professional counselor).
4. Pray, study, and receive priesthood blessings.

"Forgiveness is an ongoing process. It is a gift you give yourself. Christ offered us forgiveness . . . before we ever needed or asked for it."[25]

The Lord has said that "vengeance is mine, I will repay" (Mormon 3:15) and that Satan is the author of not forgiving (2 Corinthians 2:10–11).

Opposition

In the Book of Mormon Lehi teaches, "For it must needs be, that there is opposition in all things . . . righteousness . . . wickedness, holiness . . . misery . . . good . . . bad" (2 Nephi 2:11).

"And they taste the bitter that they may know to prize the good" (Moses 6:55–56).

"Only the soul that knows the mighty pain can know the mighty rapture."[26]

Omnipotence

God not only weeps with us as we experience pain, but He also loves and comforts us through His power. We must remember His omnipotence even when the answer to our prayer is no, or when the comfort comes in delayed or different ways than we expected.

Personal Revelation and Impressions

Personal revelation and impressions can bring healing and comfort. These spiritual impressions are provided to us by a loving

Heavenly Father through the gift of the Holy Ghost, one of the most powerful spiritual tools available.

Dennis and I had impressions that caused us to believe that we might lose Cameron. We often feared that through our neglect he would die from an accident. He regularly fell off his tricycle, and even with his helmet on he seemed vulnerable. However, we didn't anticipate that he would slip away in his sleep in a close observation hospital room with bright lights on and with Dennis and a nurse nearby.

Two years after Cameron's death, both of us were surprised how much we still missed and mourned for him. One day as I was feeling particularly sad and discouraged, I cried out in prayer, "How long will it hurt so much? Why does the pain keep coming back?" Then I heard a still small voice in my heart and mind that directed me to read in the Bible. I turned to Jeremiah 31. *A strange place to read*, I thought. I knew I hadn't read much from here before. When I got to verses 15–17, I felt the Lord was trying to comfort me and all those who have or ever will lose a loved one. "Thus saith the Lord; A voice was heard in Ramah, lamentation and bitter weeping; Rachel weeping for her children refused to be comforted for her children, because they were not. Thus saith the Lord; Refrain thy voice from weeping, and thine eyes from tears: for thy work shall be rewarded, saith the Lord; and they shall come again. . . . And there is hope in thine end, saith the Lord, that thy children shall come again."

This scripture hit me with great force and power. I realized later that this counsel was given to the mothers who were mourning for their children whom King Herod had ordered to be killed. These inspired words gave me hope and strength to endure the long earth life without two of our children.

"Fear not, let your hearts be comforted . . . waiting patiently on the Lord, for your prayers have entered into the ears of the Lord . . . all things wherewith you have been afflicted shall work together for your good" (D&C 98:1–3).

"But they that wait upon the Lord shall renew their strength; they shall mount up with wings as eagles; they shall run, and not be weary; and they shall walk, and not faint" (Isaiah 40:31).

Impressions and revelations have blessed many during adversity. Some are surprised by the answers they have received. One woman shares: "I have tried for many years to keep my temple marriage intact. I have received comfort from the Spirit and many impressions on how to do this. Even after my husband had left us and was excommunicated, I believed we would work things out and stay together. I was shocked after much fasting and prayer when I received an impression to file for divorce."[27]

Another woman, surprised by her answer, said: "My husband had been unfaithful, divorced me, remarried, and divorced again. I was shocked when I received a answer after much fasting and prayer to give him another chance and put our temple marriage back together."[28]

An unwed mother writes: "As much as I want to keep my baby, I received a strong impression that if I really love and care about him, I should place him for adoption so he can be sealed and have both a mother and a father."[29]

Faith and Hope

Having faith and hope does not mean things will always come out how we'd like. It does mean we can trust the Lord to comfort us. A Kosovo high school senior living as a refugee in Albania shared with Dennis the reason for his family's desire to return to their destroyed home in Kosovo. When Dennis attempted to return a picture of the boy's home (given to him as a thank you gift for the Church's humanitarian aid), the teen refused to take the photo back. He said, "You keep the picture so you won't forget our people. I don't need the photo because faith, hope, and Kosovo are in my heart and no man can take it from me."

In Romans 8 we read, "For we are saved by hope: but hope that is seen is not hope: for what a man seeth, why doth he yet hope for?" (v. 24). In Nephi 31 we are counseled to "press forward with a brightness of hope" (v. 20).

Faith can be a healing tool for grief recovery: "The only way to meet affliction is to pass through it solemnly, slowly, with humility and faith, as the Israelites passed through the [Red] sea. Then its very waves of misery will divide, and become to us a wall, on the right side and on the left, until the gulf narrows before our eyes, and we will land safe on the opposite shore."[30]

The scriptures also testify that not all have faith (D&C 88:118) and that faith is a gift (1 Corinthians 12:9). We all have different gifts, and we are not to judge the faithless (Romans 14:1–5).

Pilots enjoy a clear sky when they fly above the clouds, even though down below we might be buried under a blanket of dark clouds. At times our lives seem buried under a blanket of despair and discouragement, and all we can see is the darkness. The reality is, the sun is always shining. The *Son* is also always shining for us, even when we find ourselves in the black pit of despair.[31] We can have faith and tap into spiritual tools to know His power and see clearer.

The definition of faith in the Kings James Bible Dictionary reads: "Faith is to hope for things which are not seen, but are true." The apostle Paul taught, "Now faith is the substance of things hoped for, the evidence of things not seen" (Hebrews 11:1).

In the Book of Mormon we are taught that we "receive no witness until after the trial of [our] faith" (Ether 12:6). The brother of Jared displayed great faith. He progressed beyond faith when he asked the Lord to touch the stones that they might have light. His faith transcended to pure, absolute knowledge when he saw his Savior. Our faith may not be as fruitful as the brother of Jared. However, His example can encourage and even increase our faith.

After Cameron died, we hoped he would appear to us and offer comfort. When he didn't return, we found peace reading the following scripture: "Blessed are they that have not seen, and yet have believed" (John 20:29).

By faith Abraham offered up Isaac. By faith Moses refused the life offered by Pharaoh and followed God to deliver his people. By faith Joseph of Egypt survived and made the best of being kidnapped and sold by his brothers. By faith the walls of Jericho fell. By faith Joseph Smith survived emotionally and spiritually his personal trials and persecutions.

We can find strength in the parable of the mustard seed and nurture our faith: "If ye have faith as a grain of mustard seed . . . nothing shall be impossible to you" (Matthew 17:20). The mustard seed is one of the smallest seeds, yet if nourished it can grow into a large tree. After adversity we may have to start over again by replanting a tiny seed of hope. We can let our desire for faith work in us as we nourish and exercise faith (Alma 32). However, we must remember that having faith does not preclude us from experiencing grief.

Service

Service can be a healing tool that offers relief both to ourselves and others. Helping others helps us to forget our problems as we discover that there are others suffering. Sir James Barrie said, "Those who bring sunshine to others cannot keep it from themselves."[32]

Christ was an example of service during his trials: He "poureth water into a basin, and began to wash the disciples' feet, and to wipe them with a towel wherewith he was girded" (John 13:5).

He then said, "If I then, your Lord and Master, have washed your feet; ye also ought to wash one another's feet. For I have given you an example, that ye should do as I have done unto you" (John 13:14–15).

On Cameron's first birthday after his death, we were feeling really down and missing him. Someone in the ward called to see if we would take a meal in to a homebound widow. We made ourselves go, and on our way home, after delivering the food and visiting with the widow, we noticed our grief had lifted some and we felt a little better.

During our oldest son Darren's serious complications from colitis and bowel surgeries, he struggled daily for two years to regain his health. However, he felt he should keep trying to push himself to serve and work. As he offered counseling and support to others who needed him, he found peace and eventually healing for himself.

Church Attendance

We may find it difficult to attend church during and after a crisis. The hymns and lessons that once offered us comfort now may flood us with tears and remind us of our loss. For many years following Cameron's death, it was very difficult to watch the sacrament being passed without him. He had been able to pass the sacrament with the use of a special metal tray attached to the arm of his electric wheelchair. We loved watching him go row to row.

A widower said: "It's so hard to sit on the pew without my wife next to me."

A grieving woman said: "I felt like I was under glass, like everyone was staring at me, wondering how I was doing. The lessons seemed so trite compared to what I was facing."

There are also many who find increased peace and comfort at church following a crisis. "I am just loving going to church, Sunday school, Relief Society, etc.! I am soaking up every word. I am craving the spirit right now."

Eventually most of us can return to church as we find and accept our "new normal." The peace, comfort, and fellowship of worship can with time bring lasting happiness and comfort.

Sacrament Blessings

Do we only find God during times of peace, happiness, and abundance? Do we miss out on growing experiences and God's love when we look for it only in times of smooth sailing? Do we believe God loves us unconditionally? Are we only blessed when things are going well? Some experiencing adversities have asked if they are "still blessed." It is a common phrase we hear often during fast and testimony meetings. When people say, "I am blessed," what does that mean? Does it mean they have no problems in their lives or that they are focusing on the good things? If we are having a lot of adversity, can we still be "blessed"? When we ask God to bless us, are we seeking something specific, or asking for protection? Are we actually seeking His Spirit to be with us? The sacrament prayer confirms this when it says to "always remember him and keep his commandments . . . that they may always have his Spirit to be with them" (D&C 20:77, 79).

We can have His spirit with us even during adversity. We can feel "blessed" even amidst our tragedies.

Commandments

Living the commandments is a spiritual tool that can also bring comfort when we are grieving. It may seem difficult to focus on them. However, "consider on the blessed and happy state of those that keep the commandments of God" (Mosiah 2:41).

Temples

Temple attendance is a service. It also can bring answers to our prayers and provide us with comfort. Many have found the temple to be a safe and peaceful refuge during adversity.

Elder Dallin Oaks teaches, "One of the purposes of building a temple is to present to the Lord a house in which He can reveal Himself and His mysteries to His faithful children."[33]

Although some of us have had profound spiritual experiences in the temple and have felt the presence of deceased ancestors, others may not get the miracle they hoped for. One of my childhood friends recently confided in me, "I have wanted to feel the presence of my deceased son in the temple. It seems odd that others tell me they feel him there and I do not."

We don't understand all of the workings of the Spirit in the temple. There may be many reasons someone does or does not receive a particular spiritual gift. The apostle Paul tells us, "Now there are diversities of gifts . . . For to one is given . . . To another." He lists wisdom, knowledge, faith, healing, tongues, working miracles, prophecy, and discerning of spirits (1 Corinthians 12:4–11). Moroni lists additional gifts in the Book of Mormon: teaching and "the beholding of angels and ministering spirits" (Moroni 10:13). Not all people are to receive the gift of beholding angels and spirits.

Mysteries

Many of our spiritual frustrations don't end with us saying, "Okay, Lord, now I understand, and I see why these terrible things are happening to me." Rather, we must file many of life's challenges away as mysteries or something we just can't understand. Nephi taught us that God loves his children, but Nephi did not know the meaning of all things (1 Nephi 11:17).

Part of faith is knowing there are mysteries. Our natural eyes cannot see and understand all. The Greek term *mystery* means "to close the eyes or to close the mouth."

The word *mystery* appears in the New Testament twenty-four times. Paul speaks of "the mysteries of God" (1 Corinthians 4:1). "The mysteries of God's will" is found in Ephesians 1:9.

Although there are many mysteries, we are blessed as members of Christ's Church to have the restored gospel, which reveals additional spiritual knowledge.

Elder Oaks teaches, "The Melchizedek Priesthood gives us access to the mysteries of God . . . through this priesthood we receive the gift of the Holy Ghost, by which we are taught the things of God."[34]

Scriptures

When we found out that Cameron had cerebral palsy, his grandpa sent this scripture to comfort us. I have since learned the power of letting the scriptures guide, speak, and bring comfort.

> Who shall separate us from the love of Christ? Shall tribulation, or distress, or persecution, or famine, or nakedness, or peril, or sword? . . .
>
> Nay in all these things we are more than conquerors through him that loved us.
>
> For I am persuaded, that neither death, nor life, nor angels, nor principalities, nor powers, nor things present, nor things to come, nor height, nor depth, nor any other creature, shall be able to separate us from the love of God. (Romans 8:35, 37–39)

As members of the Church, we often take for granted these spiritual tools. Many of us have heard them from our childhood. Nevertheless, the most profound comfort often comes through the gifts of the Spirit. These gifts of the Spirit could include scriptures, prayer, priesthood blessings, visions, impressions, and so forth. The comfort of the Holy Ghost has given Dennis and me the strength to endure many of life's challenges. When our oldest son, Darren, was enduring surgery after surgery, impressions came as "the eyes of my understanding was opened, and the spirit of the Lord rested upon me" (D&C 138:11).

It literally felt like "the spirit like a dove descend[ed] upon" me (Mark 1:10).

Fasting and Prayer

Do we pray as fervently during good times as we do during adversity? Even the Savior seemed to turn to God more fervently during His agony and suffering,: "Being in an agony he prayed more earnestly" (Luke 22:44).

We can reach the Lord through praying, fasting, and receiving priesthood blessings. However, many struggling individuals cannot initially turn to these spiritual tools during their crisis. Some individuals following their tragedy have reluctantly shared their heartfelt disappointments: "It is so difficult to pray to a God who allowed this to happen to my family."

It's important for us to keep trying and not give up. Remember that eventually most will be able to return to their faith and reach out to God again. It will then be possible for us to tap into the power of the Holy Ghost, who is literally the Comforter. One member of the Church described it well when she wrote, "I have prayed, fasted, attended the temple, and received a priesthood blessing in hopes of being relieved of my adversity. However, my adversity still remains. Now I pray, fast, attend the temple and receive blessings to help me *endure* my adversity."

How Do We Endure to the End?

One great example of enduring is found in the story of Job. Job's many losses were intensified by the long duration of suffering he experienced:

> Time's leavening must sharpen his pain, deepen his disappointment and intensify his discouragement, to see if heightened tension would break his spirit and drive him from the Lord . . . time was assigned to chew away at Job's inner strength until he became miserable—miserable in spirit and body, so miserable in fact, that death appeared in his mind as a coveted, comforting, liberating friend. Who can imagine the state of his mind at this point? Perhaps some of us, maybe none of us.[35]

Job said he was weary of life, bitter in soul, and longing for death (Job 3:20–22; 10:1)

Enduring to the end is an important spiritual tool. Of course, most of us don't really understand the meaning of those words. We never know what challenges we might eventually have to endure or for how long.

Enduring to the end may mean a variety of things to each of

us. Sometimes accepting our adversity is the first step to enduring and healing.

Enduring is a principle of the gospel. Many righteous people have had to endure. Ten of Christ's twelve disciples were executed. Stephen was stoned. Joseph Smith, Job, and many other great men had to endure adversity. It is helpful to look to Christ as our example. He too had to experience earthly pain and suffering of His own free will: "Though he were a Son, yet learned he obedience by the things which he suffered; And being made perfect, he became the author of eternal salvation unto all them that obeyed him" (Hebrews 5:8–9).

The Prophet Joseph Smith also called out to the Lord in Liberty Jail for relief from suffering: "Oh God, where art thou? . . . Yea, O Lord, how long shall they suffer these wrongs and unlawful oppressions, before thine heart shall be softened toward them, and . . . [thou] be moved with compassion toward them?" (D&C 121:1, 3). In verse 7 the Lord told him: "My son, peace be unto thy soul; thine adversity and thine afflictions shall be but a small moment."

The Lord provided support as He continued to discuss Joseph's afflictions. However, He didn't immediately remove them. He told Joseph:

> If thou art called to pass through tribulation . . . If thou art accused with all manner of false accusations; . . . and thou be dragged to prison, . . . and the sentence of death passed upon thee; . . . if fierce winds become thine enemy; if the heavens

gather blackness, and all the elements combine to hedge up the way; and above all, if the very jaws of hell shall gape open the mouth wide after thee, know thou, my son, that all these things shall give thee experience, and shall be for thy good. The Son of Man hath descended below them all. Art thou greater than he? . . . Fear not what man can do, for God shall be with you forever and ever. (D&C 122:5–9)

After one of Darren's colon surgeries, he had to return to the hospital with a painful abscess. He was very sick and discouraged. All of his blessings had assured him that he had made the best decision in choosing to do the initial surgery. The blessings also assured him of a quick recovery. If a day is a thousand years in the Lord's time, what is a quick recovery? I recall a hospice patient asking the Lord if she could have more time (she was young). Through a personal spiritual experience, she was told she could have two extra seconds! After her death, one of our social workers did the math and felt she had received precisely the extra earth days she had prayed for.

One night after a family fast, our youngest son prayed that the blessings that had been promised to his older brother could be fulfilled. We felt renewed faith that these blessings would eventually flow down from heaven. We felt healing would eventually come, and we needed to be patient and endure. Healing was still a long time in coming, but it eventually occurred. Although Darren's brush with death was one of the hardest, most emotionally draining experiences we have endured, it was also very spiritual.

I have grown to admire those I work with in hospice. Many suffer day in and day out, week after week, month after month, wondering when death will bring relief. It's not only hard on those suffering, but also on the caregivers watching, loving, and often providing backbreaking care at the bedside. Caring for my own angel mother in our home was hard work mixed with many blessings.

Elder Maxwell taught, "When in situations of stress we wonder if there is any more in us to give, we can be comforted to know that God, who knows our capability perfectly, placed us here to succeed. No one was foreordained to fail or to be wicked. When we have been weighed and found wanting, let us remember that we were measured before and found equal to our tasks; and, therefore, let us continue, but with a more determined discipleship."[36] "If thou endure it well, God shall exalt thee" (D&C 121:8).

Patience

Paul outlines some benefits for our tribulations to help us cope. "Tribulation worketh patience; And patience, experience; and experience, hope" (Romans 5:3–4; see also D&C 54:10).

"Patience is not to be mistaken for indifference. It is to care very much, but to be willing, nevertheless, to submit both to the Lord and to what the scriptures call the 'process of time.' "[37]

Patience is a difficult attribute for many of us to obtain. "We often expect instantaneous solutions, forgetting that frequently the heavenly virtue of patience is required."[38]

"Be patient in afflictions, for thou shalt have many; but endure them, for, lo, I am with thee, even unto the end of thy days" (D&C 24:8).

Forsaken

It is helpful to remember that at times in their adversity, Job, Moses, David, Joseph Smith, Joseph in Egypt, Jesus, and many other righteous individuals have felt forsaken by God during their suffering. At times it may be difficult for us to understand why He doesn't intervene in the way we think is best or fair. Some may wonder if the Lord has forgotten them. They might say, "The Lord hath forsaken me, and my Lord hath forgotten me." And then comes the answer: "He will show that he hath not." Christ Himself then says, "Behold I have graven thee upon the palms of my hands" (1 Nephi 21:16).

When Christ was in the Garden of Gethsemane, He prayed, "Let this cup pass . . . nevertheless not as I will, but as thou wilt" (Matthew 26:39). This letting go and acceptance is a powerful example.

Covenants

We make covenants at baptism. We renew these covenants each week as we partake of the sacrament. Three of the eight covenants Alma taught at the waters of Mormon involve helping others experiencing loss and adversity:

1. Being willing to bear one another's burdens.
2. Mourning with those that mourn.
3. Comforting those that stand in need of comfort.
   (Mosiah 18:8–9)

Christ exemplified these covenants following the death of Lazarus. In John 11:35 we read, "Jesus wept." It appears that the Savior of the world, who learned obedience by the things He suffered, was willing to *mourn* with those who were *mourning* the death of Lazarus (including a distraught and somewhat frustrated Mary). The next verse makes clear the impact of the Lord's willingness to bear another's burden and stand in comfort to those present. Verse 36 reads, "Then said the Jews, behold how he loved him."

The Savior of the world knows our pain; He loves us and is there to comfort us. May God give us the strength, courage, and commitment to keep these covenants. May we be able to proclaim as Paul: "I have fought a good fight, I have finished my course, I have kept the faith" (2 Timothy 4:7).

Notes
1. Joyce and Dennis Ashton, *Jesus Wept* (Springville, Utah: Cedar Fort, Inc., 2001), 129.
2. Deanna Edwards, *GRIEVING: The Pain and the Promise* (American Fork, Utah: Covenant Communications, Inc., 1989), 151.
3. M. Russell Ballard, "You Have Nothing to Fear from the Journey," in Conference Report, Apr. 1997, 82; or *Ensign*, May 1997, 61.
4. John Taylor, *The Gospel Kingdom: Selections from the Writings and Discourses of John Taylor* (Salt Lake City: Bookcraft, 1987), 346.

5. Neal A. Maxwell, *All These Things Shall Give Thee Experience* (Salt Lake City: Deseret Book, 1979), 31.

6. Ashton, *Jesus Wept*, 135.

7. E. A. Grollman, King's College Bereavement Conference, May 1995.

8. Friedrich Nietzsche (quote public domain over 100 years old).

9. Maxwell, *All These Things Shall Give Thee Experience*, 29–31.

10. Ibid., 28.

11. Spencer W. Kimball, *Tragedy or Destiny* (Salt Lake City: Deseret Book, 1982); *Faith Precedes the Miracle* (Salt Lake City: Deseret Book, 1972), 97.

12. J. Hunt, "Hope for the Heart," Newsletter, Sept./Oct. 1996, 3.

13. Spencer W. Kimball, *Faith Precedes the Miracle*, 98.

14. Charles Meyer, *Surviving Death: A Practical Guide to Caring for the Dying and Bereaved* (Mystic, CT: Twenty-Third Publications, 1991); see also Ahston, 139.

15. Ashton, *Jesus Wept*, 141.

16. Lyndon Cook and Andrew F. Ehat, *Words of Joseph Smith* (Salt Lake City: Deseret Book), 141.

17. Merrill J. Bateman, "Living a Christ-centered Life," *Ensign*, Jan. 1999, 15; see also Ashton, 139.

18. Maxwell, *All These Things Shall Give Thee Experience*, 31.

19. Tad R. Callister, *The Infinite Atonement* (Salt Lake City: Deseret Book, 2000), 104.

20. David A. Bednar In the strength of the Lord we can do and endure and overcome all things, 10-23-2001.

21. M. Gamblin with permission to quote Dr. Paul W. Coleman.

22. Ibid.

23. Ashton, *Jesus Wept*, 146.

24. Ibid., 146–47.

25. *Church News*, Salt Lake City, Utah, 15.

26. Earl A. Grollman, *Living When a Loved One Has Died* (Boston: 1997).

27. Ashton, *Jesus Wept*, 151.

28. Ibid.

29. Ibid., 151–52.

30. Dinah M. Mulock, The Compassionate Friends Newsletter, Carrollton-Farmers Branch Chapter, Feb. 1999.

31. Ryan J. Hulbert, *The Sun Is Always Shinning* (Parma, IN: Eptic Enterprises).

32. Earl A. Grollman, *Living When a Loved One Has Died*, 90.

33. *Church News*, Oct. 31, 1992, 11.

34. Ibid.

35. Religion 302 2nd edition, prepared by the Church Educational System, The Church of Jesus Christ of Latter-day Saints SLC, Utah 1981–1982, 24–25.

36. Maxwell, Ibid.

37. Ibid.

38. Thomas S. Monson, "Peace in Our Savior," *Ensign*, June 2005, 4.

CHAPTER FOUR

Healing Our
Bodies, Minds, and Emotions

HEALING FROM A LOSS OR LIFE CHALLENGE is no
easy task. It may be the hardest work we ever do. Grief requires
us to work on our thoughts and feelings to be able to heal. It also
requires time and patience. We cannot simply make the pain of
loss and emotional injuries go away any more than we can mend a
broken leg with willpower alone.

Antoine he Saint-Exupery said, "You cannot plant an acorn in
the morning and expect that afternoon to sit in the shade of the
oak."[1]

How do we cope and heal from the hurts and challenges of
earth life? The answers are as varied as our circumstances, and
our grief is as unique as our thumbprints. In this chapter we

will identify a variety of principles and interventions designed to help us maximize our individual healing. Some coping strategies encourage us to accept and endure our adversity. Others strive to treat our symptoms and validate our suffering. Remember, suffering can be physical, emotional, cognitive, and spiritual. It is often important to find personal meaning in our suffering to maximize our healing.

According to Viktor E. Frankl, "Man is not destroyed by suffering; he is destroyed by suffering without meaning."[2]

"To live is to suffer, to survive is to find meaning in the suffering. If there is a purpose in life at all, there must be a purpose in suffering and in dying. But no man can tell another what this purpose is, each must find out for himself."[3]

"He who has a why to live for can bear with almost any how."[4]

Trying to find meaning behind what has happened may be a difficult task. It often takes a combination of grief work, prayer, and healthy thought processes to discover one's own meaning and reconciliation.

COPING VARIABLES

There are many variables that affect the way we cope and heal. We will discuss ten common ones:

1.   The type of loss or challenge we are experiencing: loss of possessions, loss of identity, and loss of relationships. Sometimes our challenges involve all four kinds of loss. Generally it is not helpful

to compare challenges by saying or thinking, "My tragedy is more difficult than yours!" However, you can compare and recognize the cumulative importance of your own losses and challenges. For instance, the loss of Dennis's and my first full-term baby and a fire that destroyed half of our dream home resulted in a more complicated grief than the death of our parents. The birth of our child with a disability was more difficult for us than our infertility and miscarriage. And all of our previous challenges combined did not compare in difficulty or prepare us for Cameron's sudden death.

2.   Another coping variable is the anticipation time. This is the amount of warning time we have (if any) to prepare for our loss or tragedy. Before their death, many patients on hospice are able to say to family members that they love them, that they're sorry, and that they'll miss them. However, others must express these important sentiments through writing or talking to the "empty chair" when their loved ones suddenly die.

3.   How close was our relationship or attachment to the person or lost object? Generally the more time, love, and energy that we have invested into a relationship, object, or particular accomplishment, the more painful will be the loss. The sadness and pain we feel after a loss is part of the love and joy we feel before the loss. We can't take the sorrow out of loss unless we take the love out of life. In hospice care, we often observe caregivers getting very attached to their loved ones. They often invest enormous amounts of compassion, love, and energy. Once the loved one is

gone, they usually experience myriad emotions.

4.   Our personalities and past coping styles contribute to how we will react and cope with life's challenges. For example, as a child I experienced separation anxiety whenever my mother went anywhere. I noticed as I grew up and experienced a variety of life's challenges, my primary reaction continued to be anxiety. How we have coped in the past often predicts how we will cope in the future. There are also personality types and disorders that can compromise someone's coping abilities. Any mental illness can also affect one's coping abilities and style.

5.   Age, gender, and maturity also influence how one responds to stress and loss. One example of gender difference is that men more often than women openly display anger when expressing loss. An example of age difference becomes obvious for many when we contrast losing a grandparent who has lived a long, happy life to losing a young child whose life has been shortened and whose future happiness on earth has not been realized.

6.   Previous losses and experiences can have a cumulative effect on one's grief and coping abilities, especially if the losses occur back to back. Multiple losses engender feelings of vulnerability and thoughts about what might happen next. When our oldest son had to have his colon removed, which resulted in serious complications, we relived Cameron's death. We probably overreacted to the event because of our vulnerability and fear that surgery would result in burying a third child.

7. Evidence has shown that our physical, spiritual, and emotional health affects our coping abilities. If someone is already vulnerable with a mental illness, they probably won't cope as well physically or emotionally and visa versa. For example, if you are rested and exercise regularly, you are not as likely to lose control of your emotions easily, and difficulties are less likely to make you irritable or angry.

8. Having a working knowledge and understanding of the grief process can help individuals cope with trials. My anxiety doesn't trigger panic like it used to because I now understand the physical process and have learned the necessary tools for coping.

9. The grief process can be complicated when our expectations are altered or shattered. If we grew up believing, "If I am good I can prevent trials," then we probably won't cope as well as the person who expected and anticipated challenges in life.

10. Our beliefs, values, and family background color our grief experience. For example, the atheist's anger is not directed at God when he is not protected from tragedy.

It may be helpful to remember that one step before becoming obsessed is being passionate. We all need to be reminded to stay balanced as we cope and strive to heal from our losses.

Elder Richard G. Scott taught, "Satan has a powerful tool to use against good people. It is distraction. He would have good people fill life with 'good things' so there is no room for the essential ones."[5]

There are many interventions and self-help tools that can aid individuals as they endeavor to cope with their personal adversities. We discussed spiritual tools in the last chapter. We will now offer additional tools as they relate to the emotional, physical, cognitive, and social dimensions of our lives.

Emotional Interventions

Acknowledging our feelings is the first step in mastering our emotions. If we don't acknowledge and honestly express our painful feelings, we deprive ourselves of the means that allow us to eventually abandon them. Because our emotions affect our physical and mental health, we need to express them in a healthy fashion. Giving voice to our fears and emotions can soften the impact. Often we don't want to feel the intense emotional pain and sadness of grief, so we ignore or shelve the feeling, hoping it will go away. Unfortunately grief usually doesn't go away, and if ignored, our painful emotions manifest themselves as physical or mental illness. What we repress may be expressed later in unhealthy ways.

Sharing and Talking

Keeping negative feelings hidden is very draining. We may not want anyone to know that we are hurt, disappointed, or angry at God because of our tragedies. We may not want our bishop or home or visiting teachers to know that we harbor hurt and negative or bitter feelings as a result of our challenges. Over time, if we continue to hide these negative feelings, we will limit our opportunity to work on them. Denial of intense unresolved emotions can lead to increased stress, depression, anxiety, or physical ailments over time.

Sharing and talking with others can soften our emotional and intellectual symptoms. We can share feelings with a friend, family member, counselor, bishop, or in a support group with others who have experienced a similar loss. Having someone listen is often all we need. One of best gifts anyone can give us is to lend an understanding, nonjudgmental listening ear. Maybe that is why God gave us one mouth and two ears.

At times we may be afraid of the intense emotions we experience. We might fear that we are going crazy or losing control. We may need a safe place to express these emotions.

Once we acknowledge our emotions, we also give ourselves permission to accept them. Acknowledging and accepting an emotion occurs most often when the emotion is expressed and validated in a safe environment. Sharing may help us face the pain and process our grief. The following four A's are interventions that can be used to facilitate our grief work:

1. *Admit* what you are feeling. Don't stuff, repress, or bury it.

2. *Analyze* the feeling. Determine where the negative or painful emotions are coming from—yourself, the

event, medical professionals, judicial system, family, church, friends, or God.

3. *Act* on the feeling through talking, crying, journaling, and working to resolve the issues. If you are angry at someone, you could write a letter expressing your concerns and issues. You don't have to mail your letter; you can burn it or save it for later. At a future time you may look at your letter and gain added insight and perspective. Try to focus on acting, not reacting. Thinking is too passive.

4. *Abandon* the intense or negative emotions. With sufficient time, active emotional expression, and grief work, most individuals can eventually abandon or soften destructive or self-incriminating emotions.[6]

If our emotions are intense and abnormal, we may need professional help.

Gratitude Therapy

Gratitude therapy is a practical self-administered tool that can be used after the four A's. When someone has acknowledged their negative emotions and worked on them, then they can focus on gratitude, as they reflect and review on the positive events and choices in their lives. Gratitude can be a powerful healing tool.

Crying

Crying is not the only way that we show our grief. However, it is often beneficial both physically and emotionally. According to Limbo and Wheeler, "Tears shed during grief have more toxins than do regular tears. Tears actually can be healing."[7]

Nearly three centuries ago, Dr. Samuel Johnson wrote, "Sorrow that hath no vent in tears, maketh the organs of the body weep."[8]

Journaling and Writing

Another self-help tool that allows individuals to process their thoughts and feelings is journaling. Studies have shown that those who write about their traumatic experiences have fewer illnesses, spend less time off work, require fewer doctor visits, and have a more positive outlook on life. As members of the Church, we are encouraged to keep personal and historic journals. However, in therapeutic journaling, we may not want to save all of our writing for our progenitors. In fact, many individuals use therapeutic writing to remove negative thoughts from their minds by writing the painful words on paper and then symbolically (or literally) destroying the pages. Through writing we can then get our painful, destructive feelings out on paper rather than harbor them inside. Repressing or stuffing our feelings can be damaging. What we resist sometimes persists. We may want to keep a loss journal for our eyes only.

This allows us to regularly record inner thoughts and feelings where they can be frequently read and evaluated. If we do keep track of what we have written, it is often helpful to review and evaluate where we were in the beginning of our experience in relation to where we have progressed after weeks or months of journaling. We should be able to see some subtle, yet significant progress in our healing, reflected as a reduction in our destructive and self-incriminating feelings.

Control versus Letting Go

When we feel vulnerable and afraid, we are more likely to attempt to overcontrol ourselves (such as through an eating disorder), others, or our environment. We may find ourselves frustrated and angry with those around us who won't do things or think the way we desire. It may cause us to feel hurt, rejected, and unloved. The more we try to control others, especially our children and spouses, the more they pull away from us.

Once we realize we don't need to overcontrol, our anxiety decreases or often leaves altogether. In addition, many of those around us will quit resisting our influence and direction. The power struggles between ourselves and others will soften as we let go. We will actually get more of what we want by letting go of the need to control.

Stephen Levine said, "When attempts at control become a prison only letting go of control will result in freedom."[9]

It may be helpful to remember that God never forces us to do anything. We are free to choose. Agency was given to us as part of His plan (Helaman 14:30; Moses 3:17; 2 Nephi 2:27).

It also helps to let go of unrealistic expectations. We then may reduce our frustration level and avoid some of the side effects of attempting to influence issues and people outside our control. Often in working with others we may need to *accept*, not *expect*.

"God grant me the grace to accept with serenity the things that cannot be changed. The courage to change the things which should be changed. And the wisdom to distinguish the one from the other."[10]

Why Me?

We may find it helpful to change our "why me?" to "what?" "when?" and "where?" We may not understand *why* something has occurred; however, we can identify *what* has happened, *what* we can do now, and *where* we can go from here. This technique will allow us to reduce our feelings of vulnerability and will empower us.

Pearl S. Buck asked herself why she had to raise a mentally disabled child. She then chose to change her views and used her positive attitude to find personal meaning: "Why must this happen to me? . . . To this there could be no answer and there was none. . . . My own resolve shaped into the determination to make meaning out of the meaningless and so provide the answer, though it was of my own making . . . her life must count."[11]

Music and Massage Therapy

Many have used a combination of massage and music to comfort those suffering. Many have discovered that touch can heal both physical and emotional pain.

Stress Management

Many individuals think that rushing and doing two or more endeavors at once (multitasking) will help them finish their tasks faster and reduce stress. However, research has shown that this technique does not always help. Trying to think of or do more than one thing at a time causes our mind to race and often creates more stress and anxiety.[12]

Stress management may mean you have to learn how to say no and then stop long enough to think before saying yes and overcommitting yourself, especially while grieving. This is hard for active Church members who want to serve others. We may have to let others serve us for a season as we rebuild our capacity to serve others once again.

Little Pleasures

It is important while enduring loss, stress, and grief to try doing the things that previously brought us happiness and pleasure. This may be as simple as ordering a pizza. After Cam's death, our family tried to do the fun things we enjoyed; however, at first nothing felt very enjoyable. With time, work, and patience we slowly started to feel better and began to once again enjoy previous activities.

Physical Interventions

EXERCISE

Physical interventions include regular exercise, which enhances the reuptake of serotonin in the brain and the release of endorphins, giving individuals a feeling of well-being. Exercise can also improve sleep if not done too close to bedtime. The type and frequency of exercise should be approved by your physician. Most professionals recommend working out four to five times per week, thirty to forty minutes per session. Exercise should begin with a warm-up and end with a cool-down period. Heart rate goals are figured based on our age. Heart rate monitors and charts are available to help you meet your goals safely.

SUNLIGHT

Sunlight also can affect brain chemistry and mood. Many individuals find that sitting near a window or walking outside regularly is helpful. Seasonal Affective Disorder (SAD) is most common in the northern states where the length of sunlight hours is diminished. Artificial sun lights are expensive but often beneficial in the treatment of SAD.

DIET

A proper diet can stabilize blood sugar and brain function, which then affects mood. Do not go for long periods without food. Complex carbohydrates (fruits, vegetables, and whole grains) have especially been shown to facilitate serotonin reuptake.

SLEEP

Proper rest is important for healing our bodies. If sleep has become a problem (a red flag for depression), we recommend that individuals try progressive relaxation, meditation, and visualization. The quality and quantity of sleep is important. During grief or stress, individuals may sleep too much or too little, either of which can produce fatigue. It is important to get back to our normal sleep cycle. Most people need seven to nine hours of sleep each night. If the following self-help sleep tools do not work, professionals may offer over-the-counter or prescription sleep aids. However, after prolonged use, some types of sleep medications may disrupt the deep sleep cycle in some individuals. For long-term insomnia, many doctors recommend a low dose of trazodone or other mild sleep aids that don't seem to disrupt the REM sleep.

A few adjustments to your bedtime routine may also help. It is important to unwind before going to bed. Arrange a quiet time before attempting to fall sleep. Try to go to sleep at the same time each night and arise at the same time each morning. Try a warm bath or milk before going to bed. Milk, meat, and other proteins contain tryptophan, a natural hormone found in the body that usually causes one to feel relaxed or sleepy.[13]

Avoid exciting television programs or novels before bedtime. Avoid napping during the day. Often we can walk or exercise instead of napping to get rid of a sluggish feeling. Daily exercise is helpful because a fatigued body requires rest at bedtime. Avoid cola or any food containing caffeine, especially before bedtime. Additionally, some medications have side effects that disrupt sleep. Some individuals report benefits from taking melatonin, a natural hormone produced in our body that promotes sleep, or herbs like valerian. These can be found at your local health food stores. However, always confer with your physician to determine the recommended doses and possible individual side effects.

MEDITATION

Relaxation and meditation may help us heal emotionally. When we are stressed at work or away from home, we can try the following quick stress management techniques: count to ten, take a deep breath, leave the situation, or take a short walk.

Relaxation and meditation can also be used as sleep tools. Instead of counting sheep, you can use concentrative meditation to focus on a word, object, or both. This prevents our mind from ruminating on problems or planning our next day's activities. Some individuals meditate best while focusing on their own relaxed breathing, a candle, flowing water, or saying a relaxing word, such as *peace, sleep,* or *calm* repeatedly. We must concentrate on the word, object, or breathing until we fall asleep. We can also use this technique when we wake up in the middle of the night or have a hard time falling back asleep.

The following relaxation technique may soften some troublesome symptoms as well as sleep. This technique involves lying flat on your back and tightening each muscle group throughout the body. Then take several deep, slow breaths through the nose, exhaling while moving the stomach or diaphragm. Next, tense, tighten, or contract each muscle group one at a time from head to toe, holding them tight and then relaxing the muscle after counting to ten. Relax each muscle group completely as you exhale. This technique can be done several times while picturing the body sinking deeper and deeper into the bed, until totally relaxed. It may be helpful to use relaxation techniques with meditation (concentrating on an image or word). Some people claim that this dimming of the sympathetic nervous system relaxes them better than taking an anti-anxiety drug. It can also slow the heart rate and lower our blood pressure. If we still cannot fall asleep, we may need to get up and do something and quit worrying about the fact that we are currently not able to fall sleep.

Cognitive/Intellectual Interventions

Some individuals may try to intellectualize the details of their situation without allowing and recognizing feelings or emotions. When they are finally ready to do their grief work, they need help transferring this knowledge from their heads to their hearts so they can experience appropriate emotions. It is usually true that we need to acknowledge, feel, and express our emotions to heal.

A cognitive tool that may be helpful is called the think/feel/act process. Some people call this process thought control, positive affirmation, or a form of cognitive therapy. When we put a positive or constructive thought in our mind, we usually feel positive emotions that bring about positive behaviors. This process can also work in reverse. Our positive actions and obedient behaviors can transcend to feeling and thinking of ourselves more favorably.

Stress reduction therapies may also help individuals who are confused, disorganized, absentminded, or disoriented.

With time, acceptance, and cognitive processing, most distressed and grieving individuals will eventually be able to let their minds rest and experience some mental closure and peace.

Social Interventions

Helping ourselves in the social dimension can be difficult. It may require getting outside our comfort zone and actually accepting another's help. It may also mean eventually reaching out to help someone else. Joining a support group is a helpful intervention for many. Sharing feelings and experiences with others who have had similar losses is often therapeutic. The power of friendship and helping others can be a powerful healing tool.

Self-esteem and Self-worth

During loss and adversity our self-esteem can appear diminished. Increasing our self esteem and, more important, understanding our self-worth can help us cope.

Self-esteem is often controlled by our actions. It is based on society's standards of what our behavior or performance should be. Self-esteem focuses on doing or having things. Because self-esteem is often shaped and controlled by the opinions of others, our goals often focus on ways to impress others.

Abraham Lincoln said, "If you do good, you feel good." Doing good things has its place. However, what about disabled, ill, or elderly individuals who can't "do"? We may need to remember and remind ourselves, "We are human beings, not human doings."

Self-esteem is often based on our accomplishments and performance. Self-worth, on the other hand, is focused more on "being" rather than our outward "doing." Self-worth is gaining confidence, peace, and happiness based on our personal attitudes and beliefs. It is not controlled by the opinions, evaluations, or approval of others. It comes from the inside out rather than the outside in. It is based on who we are and how we view ourselves. Self-worth requires understanding that our existence is not by chance, that we are created with a purpose, and that our goals and aspirations can be character-based. It requires knowing we are a children of God.

If we become so ill, disabled, or incapacitated to the point that we cannot perform in any meaningful way, we can still maintain our character and our self-worth. Stephen Covey said, "Internal security simply does not come externally."[14]

Research indicates that when we feel self-confident, we function better at work, home, and church. We have more friends and view our relationships with others more positively.

Self-love precedes our ability to love and accept others. Oftentimes, if we are critical of ourselves, we project this critical view onto others. We also tend to compare our worst qualities with others' best qualities.

Christ's love is unmerited and is not predicated solely on our performance. Our Savior died for us and loves us unconditionally. When we feel and accept His unconditional love and sacrifice, we in turn feel more self-love and self-worth. We are then free to love and forgive others as He forgives us.

"You can't always try to earn love. In its fullest state, it is given freely to you. It is the love that is there in spite of your faults that you can trust."[15]

Negative Labels

A positive self-concept is important for all of us. How we feel about ourselves influences how we respond to others and how we perceive they respond back. A poor self-image may set a negative pattern for a lifetime. It may be helpful to understand that we are in charge of our thoughts and feelings as well as our actions. In reality, no one can make us feel sad or angry. We choose to feel that way.

"Through our lives we tend to maintain many unnecessary and burdensome recurring thought and behavior patterns."[16] Often we learned these behavior patterns as children. These behaviors may initially have helped us cope with particular situations. They continue with us long after the original situation changes or no longer exists. These situations from the past can also result in our attaching negative labels to ourselves. Our children also do this. If they tell themselves something long enough, it can become a self-fulfilling prophecy that results in enduring personality beliefs and characteristics. In the Bible we read, "For as he thinketh in his heart, so is he" (Proverbs 23:7). Many of us think degrading thoughts that hinder our progress: *I've tried it before. I can't. I'm afraid. Others will laugh.*

A pessimist sees difficulty in every opportunity. An optimist sees an opportunity in every difficulty.

With work, we can dispel, or even avoid, instilling these labels. We can displace them with new positive labels.

Our lives have purpose and meaning, no matter how short or how limited. Cameron helped us recognize that all human life has value and meaning. We are all children of God with self-worth and value in spite of how limited our abilities may be.

You can test your own self-esteem by asking yourself some simple questions.

1. Am I happy when others are successful?
2. Am I comfortable meeting new people?
3. Do I hide my true feelings?
4. Am I confident with my appearance?
5. Do I like new experiences, changes, and challenges?
6. Do I recognize when I do well?
7. Do I blame others for my problems?
8. Do I accept criticism well?
9. Am I overly aggressive or inhibited?
10. Am I afraid of close relationships?

The answers for a good self-esteem would be:

1. Yes
2. Yes
3. No
4. Yes

5. Yes
6. Yes
7. No
8. Yes
9. No
10. No

President Benson lists the following tools for healing: repentance, prayer, service, work, improving our health, reading good books, blessings, fasting, good friends, good music, endurance, and setting goals and accomplishing them.[17]

Professional Therapy

Knowing when someone needs more than personal insights and self-help tools is not always easy. If someone has an abrasion, cut, or a broken arm, we physically see the wound and send them to the hospital to have it treated. We put them on antibiotics and pain medications. When someone has a broken heart and soul, we can't always see it visually; however, those suffering adversity will often tell you their emotional pain hurts more than broken bones or other physical pains they have experienced. Because emotional wounds are not always visible, individuals often fail to seek or receive the help they need. Often their body and soul have been damaged, bruised, and shattered by their loss. Professional therapy may help. There are techniques designed to address specific types of challenges. Medications have also been improved and can help a great deal. If in doubt, seek professional help and advice. LDS Family Services offers counseling and referrals to LDS professionals in your community.

When one's emotions, thoughts, or behaviors become debilitating, distorted, or exaggerated, professional help should be seriously considered. Warning signs of serious emotional distress include experiencing sadness that turns to clinical depression, anger that turns to prolonged bitterness or rage, fear that turns to anxiety or panic attacks, and guilt that turns to shame. Be aware of siblings trying to take on grown-up roles and children or parents trying to replace the deceased by imitating them. Self-pity, fear of failure or rejection, and prolonged inability to function at home, school, or work are also potential warning signs. The absence of grief can be another warning sign. Everyone is vulnerable to substituting other behaviors in place of the grief process. Substitutes may include avoidance behaviors, under or overdoing, and any type of obsession or addiction.

Different kinds of professionals with varying degrees and therapeutic specialties are available. Psychiatrists trained in medicine may view depression through a biology lens and determine a need to correct a chemical imbalance. Psychologists trained to identify the environmental and developmental influences may view pathology as a long-term consequence of childhood trauma, faulty thinking, or poor relationships. The family or marriage therapists trained in systemic thought may focus on unhealthy behaviors as a product of dysfunctional families, marriages, or gender and social inequities.[18]

Resource lists of available LDS counselors in your community are maintained by your local LDS Family Services office. Bishops are also aware, in many instances, of counselors whose therapy does not conflict with gospel standards.

Victor L. Brown said, "There is a proper place for these professionally trained specialists. The Church has an organization for this purpose. It is called LDS Family Services. There are also other faithful Latter-day Saints in public and private practice who can be called upon as a bishop feels the need."[19]

If your child is struggling, seek help from a licensed professional play therapist who has experience treating children. If you are having marital problems, seek an experienced marriage and family therapist. Therapists become licensed after several years of supervision following their graduate training. They then are required to receive hours of approved training each year thereafter. Therapeutic experience with clients, coupled with their postgraduate training, will ultimately have the greatest impact on their skills and effectiveness in therapy.

Helping Others

Many individuals wonder, "How do we help our friends, relatives, or ward members who are struggling and dealing with adversity and grief?" This scriptures give us guidance: "Weep with them that weep" (Romans 12:15).

The scriptures also give a great example of how hurtful it is when our friends and family don't offer the support we need. Job had lost nearly everything important and of value in his life when he experienced a loss that, in its own way, may have been more significant than any of the other losses. He lost the support that loyal friends and loving kinsfolk might have given had they but rallied around him in this trying season of Job's life. But, sadly, this was not to be. In his deepest need, Job, like the Savior, stood awesomely alone. "Betrayal is a cruel loss to endure. . . . The knife was twisted and turned as his friends came to his side to comfort him and instead accused him of deserving his suffering because of sin. . . . The comforters, though saying much, had misjudged his situation, and consequently said nothing relevant."[20] In Job's words, "How then comfort ye me in vain, seeing in your answers there remaineth falsehood?" (Job 21:34). "Miserable comforters are ye all" (16:1). "If your soul were in my soul's stead, I could heap up words against you, and shake mine head at you. But I would strengthen you with my mouth, and the moving of my lips should assuage your grief" (Job 16:4–5).

M. Dickson, a religious leader, explains why we desperately need support and comfort from our church leaders and ward family: "For reassurance . . . our need for reaffirmation that God still does care for us, that God is still with us and that God is still forgiving and loving and merciful. Our world has crumbled and the one constant we need to be reminded of is the constancy of God's love, as shown in Jesus Christ."[21]

A member of the Church in the midst of loss expresses a commitment to remain active and forgive those who lacked empathy or failed to express it helpfully: "I realized there were few people who could understand the intensity or duration of my grief. I felt hurt, angry, sad, and guilty on different occasions. I did not want to allow any of these emotions to drive me from my friends, family, God, faith, or church. With time, work, and patience, I, like many, found I could return with love and forgiveness to my friends, relatives, and faith family, who were unable to understand my grief. I was then able to offer help and support to others."

Some feel injured because of what they perceived God allowed or even caused to happen. To help them we must first accept and validate their feelings. When individuals tell us that they are no longer sure they believe the principles of the gospel because of the hurt and pain they are experiencing, we must listen and assure them that this can be a stage of the grieving process. If we try to rescue or correct their vulnerability and doubts prematurely, it may only cause further spiritual injury. We need to overcome our fears that these people are apostatizing and allow them time to rediscover or redefine their faith. We should refrain from prematurely pitting our testimony with theirs, or from giving them advice when they are not ready to receive it. When someone feels love and acceptance, they then feel free to explore the Spirit and rediscover their God, church, faith, and testimony.

After someone experiences a crisis, we may feel nervous the first time we see them. However, we should never ignore them or act as if nothing has happened. We should acknowledge their loss as soon as possible. A call, card, flowers, or another gesture will mean much to those suffering. A physician who lost one of his own children said that before his loss, when he would hear of a child's death, he would send a card; now he sends himself. Another way we can help the bereaved is to assist with their basic life chores. Cleaning, laundry, yard work, child care, and providing food are almost always appreciated. If a death has occurred, attending the funeral shows love, care, and concern.

Often we don't know what to say. A simple statement, "I'm so sorry you have to go through this," is usually enough. Most bereaved individuals just want you to *listen* and acknowledge and accept their pain. If they have lost a loved one, be available to talk about their loved one and reminisce. Whatever the adversity, you might ask if they would like to talk about it; however, don't pry or ask for specific details. A helpful question might be, "What aspect is most upsetting or hurts the greatest regarding your loss?" Don't worry about making them cry. Oftentimes, that is what they need to do. In *Henry VI*, William Shakespeare wrote, "To weep is to make less the depth of grief." Having someone they feel comfortable crying with can provide a beneficial release of pent-up emotions.

We must avoid telling the bereaved how they should feel, and avoid sharing our own experiences unless invited by those mourning. We should avoid saying, "We know how you feel," even when we have personally experienced similar challenges. Remember, we are all unique and may experience the same trials differently. We shouldn't contrast losses by telling about someone else in a worse situation, nor should we expect them to "get over" their loss. We can let them know we'll help them through their difficulties as long as they need us. We shouldn't expect the bereaved to call us if they need anything. They will seldom call; they are too overwhelmed and have no energy to reach out for our help. Instead, we must reach out to them for a longer duration of time than we have traditionally thought. Accept and acknowledge their feelings. Don't try to negate or minimize their loss or experiences by offering clichés. The following is a list of common hurtful clichés.

Secular Clichés

1. You are young; you will have more chances.
2. Put it behind you; get on with your life.
3. Time will heal everything. (Time alone does not heal. What one does with that time can facilitate healing [grief work].)
4. Be strong; keep your chin up.
5. Get over it; move on.

6. There are worse things.

7. Don't cry.

Clichés are not usually helpful for those struggling. We often say them because we've heard them ourselves and don't know what else to say. Even though those grieving may believe some of these clichés are true, the personal application must come from those experiencing loss themselves—not by others repeating them. Let the bereaved find their own *why's*. If a death has occurred, don't be afraid to share memories of their loved one's life.

Remember that most people do not hurt by choice; they are trying their best to cope. It will be a long, hard walk for most. It may be overwhelming and frightening for many initially to think of living with such pain.

"Do's" and "Don'ts"

+ Do let your concern and caring show. Don't expect too much and impose "shoulds" on those in mourning.
+ Do be available to listen or run errands.
+ Don't let your own sense of helplessness keep you away from those hurting.
+ Do say that you are sorry about what happened.
+ Don't avoid them because you are uncomfortable.
+ Do allow those grieving to express their feelings.
+ Don't say you know how they feel.

+ Do allow them to talk about and express what happened.

+ Don't tell them how they should feel and that they should be better now.

+ Do give special attention to siblings.

+ Don't change the subject when they want to talk about their tragedy.

+ Do allow them to do as much as possible for themselves.

+ Do respect their need for privacy.

Additional "don'ts" to be aware of:

+ Don't avoid mentioning a deceased person's name.

+ Don't try to find something positive about their tragedy; they can do that for themselves. Don't point out their blessings; they can do that for themselves.

+ Don't suggest that they should be grateful for other loved ones.

+ Don't moralize or offer theology unless invited to do so.

+ Don't say things that will intensify feelings of doubt and guilt already present.

+ Don't use clichés.

+ Don't give advice about what they should feel. There are no right or wrong feelings; they are just feelings.

+ Don't share things that were intended to be kept in confidence.

+ Don't tell them other stories of tragedy and catastrophe when they are already feeling vulnerable.

+ Don't make light of things sacred or meaningful to them.

+ Don't continually question their decisions.

+ Don't label their feelings or behavior as abnormal, childish, neurotic, and so forth.

+ Don't encourage self-destructive behavior.

+ Don't be embarrassed by tears.

Most important, remember that we can send ourselves instead of a card.

Offer Love, Time, and Support

Never hesitate to share your love and memories with the living concerning their departed loved ones. Remember, many individuals who have experienced significant loss are not grieving less over time; they're just grieving less often with the passage of time.

Some individuals seem to cope better than others. What might be a huge trial for me or someone else may not challenge you to the same magnitude. It is healing and mutually beneficial to listen to another's struggles without judgment. I didn't do this very well years ago when we moved into a new ward. We were told by several ward members about the unfriendly harshness and bitterness carried by a young mother in the ward. She had a young child diagnosed with cancer who, after suffering for more than a year, died a long and painful death. We soon had some encounters with her and agreed she was unfriendly, cold, and bitter. This added our critical judgment to that of the other ward members. This experience happened before we understood loss, suffering, and death. We know now that this woman faced many sleepless nights in which she watched her frail child cry in pain as she felt helpless to save her. A couple of years later when we buried Cameron, this woman was one of the first to send flowers, food, and eventually her listening ears and compassionate heart to wipe away the tears that few could understand.

"Comfort Those That Stand in Need of Comfort" (Mosiah 18:9)

We have buried two of our six children. Weeks after Cameron's death, Dennis ran into a good friend and neighbor while walking our dog. They talked on the corner about the fun and spiritual aspects of Cameron's life. Dave had taken the time to know Cameron and see past his limitations. When their reminiscing ended that day, Dave ended the conversation with a statement that brought great comfort. He simply said, "I want you to know, I will never grow tired of hearing you talk about Cameron." Others had shared more profound messages about death and dying that were appreciated. However, none of the counsel and expounding had the impact of these sincere words of comfort.

With time, patience, and grief work, most individuals come to understand that grief is a process; adaptation is possible, and resolution as a difficult yet worthwhile destination.

Notes

1. Earl A. Grollman, quoting Antoine de Saint-Exupery, *Living When a Loved One Has Died* (Boston: Beacon Press, 1977), 58.
2. V. E. Frankl, *Man's Search for Meaning* (New York: Simon and Schuster, 1946).
3. Ibid., 9.
4. Ibid., 85.
5. Richard. G Scott, "First Things First," *Ensign*, May 2001.
6. M. Dickson, quote from recovery seminars, Dallas, Texas 1991, 21.
7. R. K. Limbo and S. R. Wheeler, *When a Baby Dies: A Handbook for Healing and Helping* (LaCrosse Lutheran Hospital/Gunderson Clinic, Ltd., 1986), 8.
8. B. D. Rosof, *The Worst Loss: How Families Heal from the Death of a Child* (New York: H. Holt & Co., 1994), 246.
9. Stephen Levine, *A Year to Live* (New York: Bell Tower, 1997), 252.
10. Reinhold Niebuhr (quote over 100 years old).
11. Pearl S. Buck, *The Child That Never Grew* (Bethesda, MD: Woodbine House, 1950), 26.
12. Joan Borysenko, *Minding the Body, Mending the Mind* (Reading, MA: Addison-Wesley Publishing Co., Inc., 1987).
13. Robert Ornstein and David Sobel, *The Healing Brain* (New York: Guilfore, 1990), 109.
14. Stephen R. Covey, *Principle-Centered Leadership* (New York: Summit Books, 1990–91), 84.
15. M. Gamblin, American Association of Mormon Counselors and Psy-

chotherapists (AMCAP) Conference, Salt Lake City, Utah, April 1999.

16. J. M. Chamberlain, *Eliminate Your SDB's (Self-Defeating Behaviors)* (Provo, Utah: BYU Press, 1978), 1.

17. Ezra Taft Benson, in Conference Report, Oct. 1974.

18. Michael D. Yapko, *Hand-Me-Down Blues* (New York: Golden Books, 1999), 92–93.

19. Victor L. Brown, "Questions and Answers," *New Era*, Sept. 1978, 16–18.

20. Religion 302, 2nd edition, prepared by the Church Educational System (Salt Lake City: The Church of Jesus Christ of Latter-day Saints 1981–82), 25.

21. Dickson, 21.

About the Authors

Joyce Ashton is a registered nurse and certified bereavement advisor. She is currently the Director of Spiritual Care for Rocky Mountain Hospice.

Dennis is a licensed clinical social worker, former bishop, and assistant commissioner for LDS Family Services. He is currently the agency director for the LDS Family Services Centerville–Layton Utah agencies. Dennis was a guest on KRNS and KSL following the Salt Lake City Trolley Square shooting and Crandall Canyon Mine disaster. He has also appeared on *Living Essentials*.

Joyce and Dennis teach at BYU Education Week and have been broadcast on KBYU TV. They have authored two other books, *Jesus Wept* and *Loss and Grief Recovery*, and they have published online and journal articles.

Joyce and Dennis are the parents of six children, four of whom are living, and have several grandchildren.